MAKE YOUR OWN
JEWELLERY

USING FABRIC, LEATHER, EMBROIDERY, BEADS & SHELLS

MAKE YOUR OWN
JEWELLERY

USING FABRIC, LEATHER, EMBROIDERY, BEADS & SHELLS

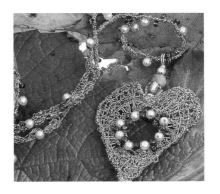

OVER 40 INSPIRING STEP-BY-STEP PROJECTS FOR CREATING ALL KINDS OF STYLISH BANGLES, BROOCHES, EARRINGS, RINGS, NECKLACES, HAIR ACCESSORIES, TRINKET BAGS AND BOXES, SHOWN WITH OVER 400 STUNNING PHOTOGRAPHS

EDITED BY **ANN KAY**

southwater

This edition is published by Southwater, an imprint of Anness Publishing Ltd, Hermes House, 88–89 Blackfriars Road, London SE1 8HA; tel. 020 7401 2077; fax 020 7633 9499

www.southwaterbooks.com; www.annesspublishing.com

If you like the images in this book and would like to investigate using them for publishing, promotions or advertising, please visit our website www.practicalpictures.com for more information.

UK agent: The Manning Partnership Ltd; tel. 01225 478444; fax 01225 478440; sales@manning-partnership.co.uk

UK distributor: Grantham Book Services Ltd; tel. 01476 541080; fax 01476 541061; orders@gbs.tbs-ltd.co.uk

North American agent/distributor: National Book Network; tel. 301 459 3366; fax 301 429 5746; www.nbnbooks.com

Australian agent/distributor: Pan Macmillan Australia; tel. 1300 135 113; fax 1300 135 103; customer.service@macmillan.com.au

New Zealand agent/distributor: David Bateman Ltd; tel. (09) 415 7664; fax (09) 415 8892

Publisher: Joanna Lorenz
Editorial Director: Helen Sudell
Editor: Ann Kay
Designer: Nigel Partridge
Production Controller: Claire Rae

Previously published as part of a larger volume,
Create Your Own Jewellery

Images on front cover: Wrapped earrings, p42–3; Horse brooch, p65–6; Heart hatpin, p60–1.

1 2 3 4 5 6 7 8 9 10

ETHICAL TRADING POLICY

At Anness Publishing we believe that business should be conducted in an ethical and ecologically sustainable way, with respect for the environment and a proper regard to the replacement of the natural resources we employ.

As a publisher, we use a lot of wood pulp to make high-quality paper for printing, and that wood commonly comes from spruce trees. We are therefore currently growing more than 500,000 trees in two Scottish forest plantations near Aberdeen – Berrymoss (130 hectares/320 acres) and West Touxhill (125 hectares/305 acres). The forests we manage contain twice the number of trees employed each year in paper-making for our books.

Because of this ongoing ecological investment programme, you, as our customer, can have the pleasure and reassurance of knowing that a tree is being cultivated on your behalf to naturally replace the materials used to make the book you are holding.

Our forestry programme is run in accordance with the UK Woodland Assurance Scheme (UKWAS) and will be certified by the internationally recognized Forest Stewardship Council (FSC). The FSC is a non-government organization dedicated to promoting responsible management of the world's forests. Certification ensures forests are managed in an environmentally sustainable and socially responsible basis.

For further information about this scheme, go to www.annesspublishing.com/trees

© Anness Publishing Ltd 2007

A CIP catalogue record for this book is available from the British Library.

Contents

Introduction

Everyone loves jewellery, whether to wear or to give, and it seems to fulfil a basic human desire. Personal ornaments are among the oldest artefacts found by archaeologists, and jewellery has always been just as significant for its meaning as for its beauty and worth. It's a universal symbol of wealth, power, love and desire. Yet the word "jewel" is derived from a Latin word for a plaything, and jewellery can certainly also be a source of pleasure and amusement. While you might keep family heirlooms such as pearls and

diamonds in the bank, the pieces you choose to wear every day have a different kind of value. They're a daily delight and a perfect way to express your personality, especially if you've made them by hand.

This book takes a practical look at the art of making jewellery and concentrates on pieces that don't require specialist skills or costly raw materials. While it does include some beautiful, delicate bead and embroidery work, there are also surprising and original ideas for turning everyday materials such as shells, leather and felt into characterful jewellery, transformed by clever techniques. You can even discover how to

create glittering filigree confections using your sewing machine.

Beautiful photographs of 45 finished pieces will inspire you, whether you follow the detailed step-by-step instructions to reproduce the designs exactly or use the techniques described to develop

your own variations. The projects range from simple brooches and necklaces that complete beginners can manage to sophisticated machine techniques. The pliers symbols indicate the level of difficulty, so you can tackle the simplest examples of each technique first. As well as the jewellery – from

earrings and necklaces to hairslides and brooches – you'll find beautiful containers to keep your jewellery in. They look attractive on your dressing table, or are a wonderful way to present a piece of handmade jewellery. Other unusual gifts include the bride's garter and the jewellery roll.

Jewellery Fittings

To make your own jewellery, you need a variety of fittings, such as necklace clasps, brooch pins, chains and earring wires. The term "findings" is the name given to the many different parts used to fasten or link jewellery.

The best-known findings include jump rings, the small metal rings used in all kinds of ways to link different parts of jewellery items (for example, to join the end of a string of beads to a clasp) and butterfly backs, for holding studs in place in pierced ears.

If you become very adept at metalwork, you might choose to make most of these kinds of things yourself, but in the meantime certain craft stores, and some jewellery stores, sell an enormous range of fittings to make jewellery-making really easy. You can also obtain fittings from the many companies selling them to the trade; most of these operate mail order schemes and have easily accessible websites.

Fabric and Leather

Textiles of all kinds offer endless scope for creating original necklaces, brooches and hair decorations, and you may find you already have nearly everything you need to explore these ideas: scraps of pretty fabrics or leather, shimmering ribbons and a scattering of beads. Really unusual pieces can be created using the crafts of feltwork, ribbonwork, ragwork and leatherwork, producing exciting, textural works of wearable art.

Made by turning wool fibres into solid fabric, felt is an ideal jewellery material as it is lightweight and can be created in any number of lovely colours. Wool can also be mixed with fibres such as silk and mohair.

Feltwork Materials

Carded sliver

This wool is commercially sorted into fibres of the same length, bleached and carded into a long rope ready for spinning or felting. You can buy it pre-dyed or dye it yourself.

Commercial felt

Felt pieces are now available from general craft suppliers in a wide range of colours.

Dye

Acid dyes – so-called because an acid such as vinegar must be added to the dye bath – are ideal for wool. They need very hot water to work well, but give good colourfast results.

Felteen

This is a clear fabric stiffener commercially used in the making of felt hats. PVA glue diluted with water can also be used to stiffen felt, but will leave a surface sheen.

Glass beads

Beads in a wide range of sizes and shapes can be stitched directly on to felt items as decoration.

Jewellery findings

Standard findings are easily attached to felt pieces, using either thread or epoxy glue. Use nylon-coated jewellery wire to thread felt beads.

Thread

Ordinary sewing thread can be used in a sewing machine to create embossed lines or relief effects on thin felt. As well as being used for embroidered decoration, metallic thread can be trapped under a thin web of fibres and felted into the fabric.

Uncarded fleece

Fleece needs to be cleaned, dyed and carded, but it gives greater scope for experimentation than prepared sliver. Felt is best made from wool with a staple or fibre length of 2.5–5cm/1–2in: longer fibres will tangle. The ideal wool for feltmaking is Merino.

Much of the equipment needed for feltwork can be improvised; felt made from carded sliver requires no specialist items. The most important thing is a cloth or mat in which to roll the felt.

Feltwork Equipment

Bamboo mat

Rolling the fleece on a bamboo or sea-grass beach mat increases friction and speeds the felting process.

Craft (utility) knife

A very sharp blade is essential for cutting cleanly through felt balls.

Drum carder

This will card a large amount of wool quickly, but is an expensive piece of equipment, only really necessary if you do a lot of feltmaking.

Hand carders

Once you get into the rhythm, wool can be carded by hand quite quickly. If you have no carders, use pre-carded sliver, which can be teased open with your hands.

Needles

For sewing felt choose "straw" or "milliner's" needles, which are extra long with small eyes that do not create a bulge in the shank. A needle with a large eye and a sharp point is useful for threading felt balls and beads.

Scissors

To cut through felt smoothly scissors need to be really sharp. Dressmaker's shears are needed for cutting out flat pieces of felt, and small sharp-pointed scissors for embroidery and beadwork.

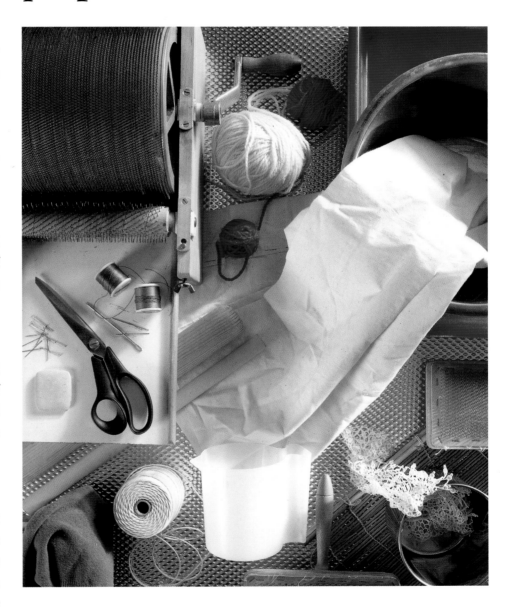

Soap flakes

All soap will make felt, but some kinds have properties less advantageous to the feltmaker. For example, washing powder is too harsh and hand soap washes out too quickly. Pure soap flakes are most suitable as they are very mild and easy to rinse out.

String

Any string that will not disintegrate in hot water or stain the wool when wet can be used to hold carded wool in hanks during the washing and dyeing processes. Cotton string is best as knots will not slip and it can be re-used many times.

The transformation of a mass of loose wool fibres into a solid piece of felt is a mysterious and intriguing process, as it requires only the action of heat, moisture and friction, aided by soap.

Feltwork Techniques

Making Felt Balls and Beads

A small ball will take about 20–30 minutes. When the wool is fully felted the ball will have shrunk considerably and will bounce if thrown hard on to a table.

Dyeing Wool

The felt jewellery in this book has been made using carded sliver, which is wool that has been industrially cleaned and carded. This can be bought pre-dyed, or bleached ready for dyeing.

1 Twist a length of carded wool into a tight ball. If the finished ball is to be cut in half, for example when making buttons or earrings, use several colours to achieve a marbled effect.

2 Cover the ball in another layer of carded wool, wrapping it around evenly. Keep the ball in your hand to stop it falling apart. Dip the ball in hot, soapy water, squeezing it to wet it through to the middle.

1 To dye fleece or wool sliver, follow the dye manufacturer's instructions to make up a dye bath of hot water and lower the wool into it.

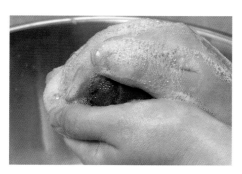

3 Roll the ball gently in your cupped hands. As the fibres begin to felt, increase the pressure steadily and dip the ball back in the water from time to time. When the wool has fully felted, rinse out the soap and leave to dry. The ball may be put in a spin drier or on a radiator to speed this up.

4 To make a bead of a different shape, such as an egg-shape, squeeze the ball into the form you need once the outer layer has hardened but while the core is still soft. Complete the bead as before, without losing the shape.

2 Slowly bring the bath to the boil and allow to simmer for an hour. Do not stir or prod the wool, as this will cause felting. Allow the dye bath to cool before lifting out the wool and drying it in a warm airy place, away from direct heat.

Ribbons come in an appealing variety of colours and textures, from silks and velvets to glittering metallics and exotic patterns. Basic sewing equipment is all you need to transform them into exquisite ornaments.

Ribbonwork Materials

Ribbons

As ribbon weaving keeps pace with technology, an ever-wider range becomes available. The individual project will dictate the kind of ribbon you need, and your choice should depend not only on colour and pattern but on the finished effect you require. For example, a basic single-loop bow can be made from any type of ribbon and still look stunning, whereas more elaborate looped and gathered designs may demand soft satin or wire-edge ribbon to look really effective.

Woven-edge ribbons – These have selvedges down each side; they are often made to very high standards and are washable: each reel should carry full details of crease resistance and colour fastness. They are primarily intended for use on clothing and soft furnishings. A huge variety is available, including taffeta, moiré, woven checks, and single- or double-faced satin. High-quality embroidered ribbons can be expensive, but are effective in small amounts when used in jewellery-making. The narrowest widths of satin ribbon are suitable for threading beads. They can also be used for rich embroidery, or as delicate streamers to trim hair decorations.

Craft ribbons – These are purely decorative and offer interesting surface weaves and a variety of wired edgings.

A satin-stitched edge, often encasing a fine wire, is known as merrow edging. Wire-edge ribbons can be moulded into stable loops for creating bows and flowers.

Glue

PVA (white) glue can be used to fix your ribbon designs in place. A glue gun is not absolutely essential but makes it easier to apply glue with speed and accuracy.

Wire

If you are making stemmed ribbon roses as part of your jewellery design, then you will need florist's stub wire to maintain stiffness in the stems. Flexible florist's wire is wrapped around the base of the flower to secure the shape properly. Remember that you must avoid using scissors to cut the wire, however thin, as this will ruin the blades instantly – always use wire cutters.

With a little practice in manipulating ribbons into loops and bows, and a few basic sewing techniques, you can turn these simple strands of colour into exquisite artefacts.

Ribbonwork Techniques

Wire-edge Ribbon Rose

This quick and easy decoration is perfect for attaching to a hairslide (barrette) or brooch. For a medium-sized flower you need about 90cm/1 yd of 39mm/1½in ribbon. Artificial rose leaves can be added by binding them to the stem using green florist's tape (stem wrap).

1 Tie a knot in one end of the ribbon. From the other end, pull the wire from one side of the ribbon, creating gathers.

2 Using the knot to form the centre of the flower, wind the gathered edge around its base.

3 To add a stem, twist one end of a florist's stub wire around the base of the rose, then wrap the exposed ribbon wire around the top of the stem.

4 Tease the ungathered ribbon edge into petal shapes. Cover the wire stem with green florist's tape (stem wrap), adding artificial leaves if you wish.

Right: *The shading of ombré taffeta wire-edge ribbon contributes to the realistic appearance of these roses.*

Ribbon Bows

The classic hand-tied bow needs no stitching or wiring, but both can be used to produce a perfect bow that won't come undone.

Hand-tied Bow

1 Fold a length of wire-edge or traditional soft ribbon in half to find the centre point. Fold each half of the ribbon across the centre to make two loops and two tails. Hold the ribbon layers together securely and bind a piece of fine florist's wire tightly around the centre.

2 Conceal the florist's wire by wrapping a short piece of matching or contrasting ribbon around the centre of the bow. Secure it with either glue or a couple of small handstitches at the back. Trim the tails of the bow neatly if necessary and gently pull the bow loops and trimmed tails into the required shape.

Multi-loop Bow

1 Find the centre of a length of ribbon as before and fold the ribbon into the desired number of loops, making sure that you keep all the loops the same size and that you hold the centre of the bow firmly in place. There should be an even number of loops on each side of the centre.

2 Secure the mid-point of the folded loops and form the centre of the bow by binding with a length of fine florist's wire. Conceal the wire with a short piece of matching ribbon and glue or stitch it in place at the back. Trim the ribbon ends and tease out the loops attractively.

Ribbon Embroidery

Embroidering small-scale projects using narrow ribbon creates intricate textural effects.

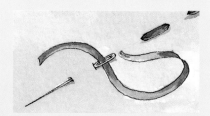

Running stitch is used both decoratively and to join or gather fabric. Pass the needle in and out, keeping the stitches small and even. Push the fabric along the thread to gather it.

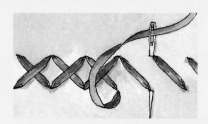

For cross stitch, work a row of diagonal stitches from right to left, then complete the crosses by stitching from left to right.

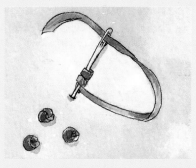

To make a French knot, bring the thread up through the fabric and twist the needle around the ribbon two or three times. Insert the needle just beside the point where it came up and pull the thread down through the twists to form a knot.

Since the essence of ragwork is its economical use of recycled fabrics, the materials and equipment needed are minimal. The most unlikely materials, even including plastic bags, can be used to great effect.

Ragwork Materials and Equipment

Hook
A tapering, sharp-ended brass hook with a turned wooden handle is pushed through the hessian to make a large hole, through which the fabric is hooked. A large crochet hook can also be used to hook small pieces.

Hoop
Hessian needs to be stretched taut on a frame for ragwork; an embroidery hoop is suitable for small projects such as jewellery.

Plastic bags and foils
Strips of plastic sheet, such as carrier bags, can be used with or instead of fabrics. Add sparkle with foil-backed crisp (chip) packets and gift wrap.

Scissors
You need two pairs: sharp dressmaking shears for cutting fabrics and pile and another pair for paper, foil and plastic, as these will blunt the blades.

Sewing materials
Findings such as brooch backs and earring clips can be stitched to ragwork pieces, and backing fabric can be slip-stitched in place. Embroidery thread (floss) is used for decorative finishes.

Wire
Thin wire is useful to stiffen the ragwork for sculpted pieces.

Adhesives
Latex carpet adhesive can be used to back finished pieces of ragwork. Use clear impact adhesive to attach backing fabric and strong epoxy resin glue to secure jewellery findings.

Fabrics
Cotton – Jersey fabrics, such as old T-shirts, fray very little and make excellent looped surfaces. Printed shirts and dresses are also ideal.
Nylon – Thin jersey (such as coloured tights) makes a fine-textured surface.

Felt
Black felt makes a smart backing fabric to finish pieces of jewellery such as brooches and earrings.

Hessian (burlap)
Old sacking was the traditional recycled foundation for hooked rag rugs but nowadays hessian, made from jute, can be bought by the metre or yard. It is strong and pliable and the threads open and close easily when hooking. It is available in different weights – 250g/9oz is perfect for ragwork.

All ragwork involves cutting fabric into strips but several techniques can be used to work them into the finished item. Use contrasting materials and surface treatments to create a wide range of textures.

Ragwork Techniques

Hooking   This is the commonest and most versatile technique, in which fabric strips are hooked through hessian (burlap). They can be left as a loop pile or sheared to create a cut pile surface. A combination of the two surfaces gives a sculpted, three-dimensional effect.

1 With the hessian in a frame, push in the hook and feed on a loop of fabric. Pull the hook back, bringing the end of the strip to the top. Push the hook back in 1–2 warp threads away and then feed a loop on to the hook as before.

2 Pull the hook back to make a fabric loop approximately 1cm/½in high. Repeat in order to create rows of loops to cover the hessian. When you reach the end of a strip, pull it through to the top. Trim to the same height as the loops.

3 To create a cut pile surface, pull the fabric through in loops as before but hook them to a height of approximately 2cm/¾in. When the area is filled, shear across the tops of the loops with a large pair of scissors.

Backing and Finishing   Once the ragwork is complete the edges of the hessian need to be neatened and the back covered. Backing jewellery pieces with a soft fabric such as felt will prevent the hessian irritating the skin.

1 Trim around the finished piece to leave a hessian border at least 2cm/¾in wide. Spread latex adhesive all over the back and leave to dry for 3–5 minutes, then fold in the edges.

2 Cut any excess hessian away at the corners to make the underside as flat as possible.

3 Cut a piece of felt slightly larger than the ragwork. Pin around the edge and slip-stitch in place, turning in the excess felt as you go.

Leather offers a distinctively unusual material for jewellery. Leatherwork is a skilled craft, but small-scale jewellery projects can be accomplished using little more than basic sewing materials and equipment.

Leatherwork Materials and Equipment

show through the colour. Treat leather decorated in this way with beeswax before polishing it.

Needles

Leather needles – Embroidery needles may be sturdy enough for very fine skins, but leather needles are better able to pierce thicker hide.

Glover's needles – These have a three-sided point that acts as a cutting edge. They are available in a range of sizes.

Punch

A rotary leather punch is used to make holes, both decorative and functional. Choose a good-quality punch with replaceable cutting tubes.

Adhesives

PVA (white) glue can be used to stick pieces of leather together if the surfaces are roughened to provide a key. Use epoxy resin glue to attach jewellery findings.

Leather

Hide can be bought by the full skin or in cut sections that are ideal for small projects. Skins are available natural or pre-dyed in a wide range of different finishes and colours, including metallics. Skiving leather is a natural

undyed hide that has been pared down in order to make it thin enough for moulding.

Leather stain

Stains are water- or alcohol-based. Unlike dyes or paints, which colour the surface, stains penetrate the skin.

Felt-tipped pens

For small items, coloured decorations can easily be added to natural leather using permanent felt-tipped pens. Translucent pens allow the grain to

Scissors, knives and shears

Special leather scissors are sturdy with rounded ends. Small shapes can be cut using a craft knife and cutting mat. Use pinking shears to add a decorative edging to lightweight leathers.

Sewing thread

Linen thread is used for most leatherwork, and is waxed to help it slip through the skin easily. Cotton thread may be strong enough for fine skins, and embroidery thread (floss) can be added for decoration.

It's a good idea to practise any techniques for shaping or decorating leather on scraps or offcuts of a similar colour and thickness before using them on your chosen piece of skin.

Leatherwork Techniques

Punching

A row of punched holes, perhaps combined with a pinked edge, makes an effective decoration for fine leather.

It's best to place a scrap piece of thick leather under the item you are punching to protect the cutting tubes. If you need to get to a point beyond the reach of the punch, try folding over or gathering the leather.

Moulding Leather

When dampened, vegetable-tanned, undyed leather can be moulded into shapes that it retains when dry.

Thick leather needs to be soaked to soften the fibres, but small thin pieces need only be moistened with a sponge and warm water. Press the leather into the desired shapes using your fingers.

Dyeing Leather

Protect the work surface and work in a well-ventilated area if you are using alcohol-based dye. The leather must first be cleaned so that it is completely free of grease, as this can resist the dye.

1 To clean the leather, make a solution of oxalic acid (5ml/1 tsp to 600ml/1 pint water) and rub over the surface using a soft cloth. Leave to dry. Dampen the leather with a sponge then apply the dye with a cloth, working over the surface in a circular motion.

2 It is easier to obtain an even colour if you apply several layers of dye. Apply polish to seal the surface and make the colour permanent.

This bright necklace is fun to wear and easy to make. The large beads are very light and will not weigh you down. Experiment with different shapes of beads, and try mixing colours to create a marbled effect.

Felt Bead Necklace

you will need

50g/2oz fleece, in carded slivers, in various colours

soap flakes

bowl

2 crimp beads

nylon-coated jewellery wire

necklace clasp

small pliers

large needle

1 Divide the fleece into bundles to make 19–21 beads, each containing two or three colours. Wind and twist each bundle into a tight ball, keeping it in your hand to stop it falling apart.

2 Dip each of the balls that you have just made in hot, soapy water. Now squeeze and roll each ball in your hands to felt the fibres until you can feel that the ball is hard all the way through. Rinse each bead under a hot tap then a cold one, and allow to dry. (A spin dryer will help speed up the drying process.)

3 Lay the beads out in the order in which you want to thread them. Thread a crimp bead on to the nylon-coated wire and then one half of the clasp. Turn the wire back through the crimp bead and crush the bead, using a small pair of pliers, to secure the wire.

4 Thread the wire on to a large needle then push this through all the beads to thread them on to the wire. Attach the other half of the necklace clasp as described in step 3.

Though this bracelet has a chunky look it is light and soft to wear. You can vary the end result by adding embroidery, sewing on beads or artificial flowers, or incorporating other yarns under the surface of the felt.

Felt Bracelet

you will need

40g/1½oz fleece in carded slivers, three colours

string

heavy weight

soap flakes

bowl

scissors

needle and matching sewing thread

1 Divide each length of fleece in half. Make the wool up into two plaits, each of the three colours, leaving two additional strands unplaited. Tie the two plaits and the two strands together at one end with string and attach the string to a heavy weight. Twist the plaits and strands tightly together and tie the other end of the twist securely with string.

2 Wet the wool thoroughly with hot, soapy water, keeping the plaits and strands in a twist. Rub the length of the fibres with plenty of soap, using one hand to keep the twist pulled taut against the weight all the time. The fibres will soon felt together, after which the twist will not unwind.

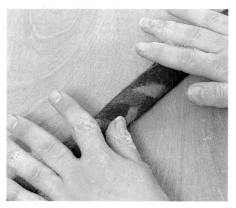

3 When the wool has felted on the outside, untie the string from the weight and roll the wool "sausage" firmly on the worktop to felt the fibres in the middle.

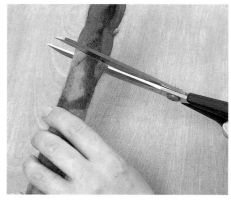

4 While the sausage is still flexible, cut off the ends tied with string. Wrap the felt around your wrist to check the fit and make sure that it will go over your hand when the ends are joined up. Trim down as required.

5 Stitch the two ends together using a long needle and strong thread. Take the thread from end to end inside the felt as well as stitching around the edges, to make the join very strong.

6 Felt the bracelet again in hot water and soap to shrink the inside curve and hide the stitches at the join. Rinse and allow to dry.

Felt brooches were popular in the 1930s and 1940s, when their bold colours gave a lift to a dull winter coat or plain hat. This design uses a thinner commercial felt than would have been available then.

Felt Flower Brooch

you will need

tracing paper, pencil, card (stock) and
scissors (for templates)
10 x 5cm/4 x 2in commercial
felt pieces, one each of pink,
mauve and orange
14.5 x 3cm/5¾ x 1¼in felt pieces,
one each of yellow and three
shades of green
scissors for cutting felt
needle and matching sewing thread
45cm/18in string
sewing machine
brooch back

1 Trace the templates from the back of the book. Transfer to the felt and cut out two flower shapes each in pink, mauve and orange, and four leaves in various shades of green.

2 Put the petals together in contrasting pairs. Now cut a fringed edge along three strips of yellow felt for the flower centres. Roll them up and place them in the centre of the paired petals.

3 Stitch the flower centres in place. Pinch the backs of the petals, and stitch through all the layers to give the flowers more shape.

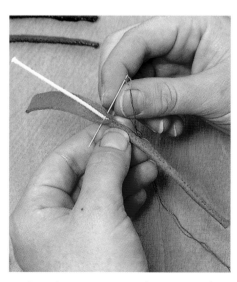

4 Cut the string into three 15cm/6in lengths, then slip-stitch a thin strip of green felt around each length to create the stalks.

5 Using a sewing machine, satin-stitch along the centre of each leaf to make a rib. Sew the four leaves together in a fan shape. Fold the stalks in half and sew them to the leaves. Then sew the flowers to the leaves over the folds of the stalks.

6 Now turn the brooch over and stitch the brooch back on very firmly, right in the centre.

A felt ball cut in half to reveal an intricate pattern makes a delightful pair of earrings. Cutting through the ball to reveal the marbled colours is so exciting it will probably prompt you to make more than one pair.

Marbled Earrings

you will need

5g/⅛oz fleece, in carded slivers, various colours

soap flakes

bowl

craft (utility) knife

felteen hat stiffener or PVA (white) glue

epoxy resin glue

earring posts and butterfly backs

1 Make a ball by twisting and wrapping two or more colours of fleece together. The more twists, turns and colours you use in the middle of the ball, the more intricate the resulting pattern will be. Dip the ball in hot, soapy water and squeeze and roll it to felt the fibres all the way through. When hard, rinse under a hot tap then a cold one.

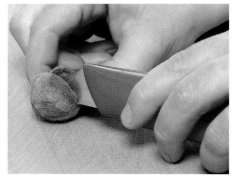

2 Leave the ball until it has dried out completely, then cut it in half using a craft knife. The pattern should stay in place; if the ball has not been felted all the way through, the middle will bulge out at this point.

3 To make the felt really hard, dip it in felteen hat stiffener. The felt must be absolutely dry as water reacts with the stiffener and will make a cloudy white film on the surface. An alternative is to dip the felt in PVA glue diluted with water, although this leaves a shiny surface.

4 Mix up a little two-part epoxy resin glue according to the manufacturer's instructions and use it to attach an earring back to the domed back of each earring.

These beaded felt buttons are ideal for a special cardigan or jacket, but they could also be used as eye-catching ornaments, or threaded on a leather thong, knotted at intervals, to make a necklace.

Acorn Buttons

you will need

6g/¼oz fleece in carded slivers, brown and gold

soap flakes

bowl

craft (utility) knife

needle and strong button thread

1,000 small faceted glass beads

polyester thread

1 Divide the brown and gold fleece into three and make each into three balls by dipping them in hot, soapy water and rolling in your hands. For the brown fleece, keep rolling and felting the balls until they are very hard and bounce when dropped.

2 For the gold fleece, squeeze and roll the balls as before but when they are beginning to go hard, distort them into the shape of rugby balls with your fingers. Rinse all the balls thoroughly in hot, then cold water.

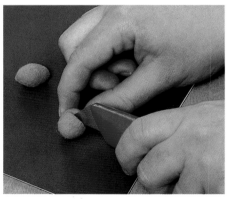

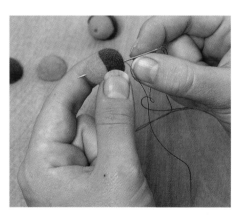

3 Leave the balls to dry out completely, then cut each one in half using a sharp craft knife. When halving the gold rugby balls, cut across the narrow width.

4 With their cut faces together, sew the gold half balls to the brown half balls using strong button thread. Make a stitch straight through the middle of each acorn and back, and pull the thread tight to form a small dimple at the top of each gold ball.

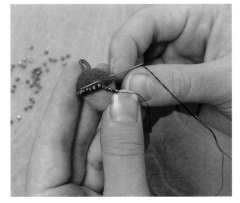

5 With the thread emerging from the base of the brown ball, make three small loops, one on top of the other, and use these as the foundation of a buttonhole shank.

6 Use polyester thread to sew beads round the rim of each acorn cup then spirally down to the shank to cover the cup. Sew the beads in groups of six: back-stitch three beads and catch down the thread before bringing the needle back out at the sixth bead.

Patterned ribbons can be irresistible and these tubular beads are an excellent way to make a feature of them. Mix and match the designs with coordinating small beads to make a necklace of subtle richness.

Ribbon Beads

you will need

white card (stock)

pencil

ruler

scissors

39cm/15in wire-edge patterned ribbon, 50mm/2in wide

PVA (white) glue

needle and matching sewing thread

round beads, 1.5cm/⅝in diameter

plastic-coated garden wire

75cm/30in toning ribbon, 3mm/⅛in wide

tubular beads

small gold beads

necklace clasp

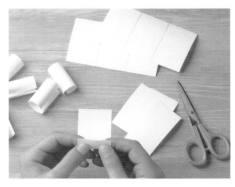

1 Cut six 7 x 4cm/2¾ x 1½in rectangles from the card and roll into tubes starting from one of the narrow ends.

2 Cut six 6.5cm/2½in strips of patterned ribbon, selecting the pattern area that you want to use along the ribbon. Now glue one end of each piece of ribbon on to the outside end of each tube of paper. Allow to dry completely.

3 Fold over the other end of the ribbon by 5mm/¼in. Roll the ribbon around the tube so that the edges of the ribbon meet. Stitch down the join. Push the wired edges of the ribbon into each end of the tube.

4 Apply glue to both ends of each covered tube and press a bead on to each end. Hold the beads in place while the glue dries by threading a piece of wire through each tube and bending the ends over.

5 Thread the ribbon-covered tubes on to the narrow ribbon, arranging round and tubular coloured beads and small gold beads in between them.

6 Thread a clasp on to the ends of the ribbon. Fold each ribbon end back on itself and stitch down, wrapping the thread over the stitching. Knot the end of the ribbon and wrap again with thread to cover the knot. Secure the thread firmly before cutting it off.

Romantic ribbon roses in harmonizing colours, framed by a circle of lace and trimmed with delicate streamers, create a charming posy effect for this hair ornament, which is ideal for a young bridesmaid.

Rose Hair Accessory

you will need

80cm/32in dark rose-pink ribbon, 2.5cm/1in wide

scissors

needle and matching sewing thread

40cm/16in warm beige ribbon, 2.5cm/1in wide

50cm/20in pale pink ribbon, 12mm/½in wide

30cm/12in cream ribbon, 10mm/⅜in wide

60cm/24in dark rose-pink ribbon, 6mm/¼in wide

30cm/12in dark pink ribbon, 6mm/¼in wide

50cm/20in cream lace, 4cm/1½in wide

10cm/4in oval hairslide (barrette)

PVA (white) glue

20cm/8in each pale green, dark rose-pink and beige ribbon, 3mm/⅛in wide

1 Cut the 2.5cm/1in-wide dark rose-pink ribbon in half to make two large ribbon roses. Have a needle and thread ready for the final step. Fold the ribbon at a right angle, two-thirds along its length, and hold in place firmly.

2 Pass the long end under the triangular fold and hold with your other hand. Pass the short end under and hold, then continue to make concertina folds to the end of the ribbon.

3 Hold the two ends together, and gently grip with the thumb and forefinger of one hand. Carefully draw up the long end. This ruffles the ribbon and forms the rose petals.

4 Secure the rose with stab stitches, being sure to pass through all the layers, then trim the ribbon ends. Make a second dark rose-pink rose, one warm beige, three pale pink, two cream, one small dark rose-pink and three dark pink roses in the same way.

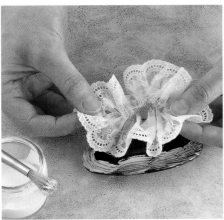

5 Gather the lace along its straight edge and draw it up in an oval shape to fit on to the hairslide. Tucking the raw ends neatly under, glue in place with PVA glue and leave to dry.

6 Arrange the ribbon roses inside the gathered lace and stick in place, one at a time, with the larger roses towards the centre framed by the smaller ones.

7 Cut several 4cm/1½in lengths of the green ribbon and stitch the ends together to form loops. Sew these between the roses around the outer edge. Make loops and streamers from the rest of the narrow ribbons and attach as shown.

Exuberant ribbon roses make a perfect hair accessory to go with a special party dress. Choose lavish satin and silk organza ribbons in shades that tone with your outfit and set off the colour of your hair.

Ribbon Rose Hairband

you will need

60cm/24in tartan ribbon,
6cm/2¹⁄₂in wide
needle and matching sewing thread
scissors
1m/1 yd each plain and gold-edged
green organza ribbons,
4 cm/1¹⁄₂in wide
satin-covered padded hairband
6 x 38cm/15in lengths of organza and
satin ribbons, 4cm/1¹⁄₂in wide

1 Make the central rose first. Fold one end of tartan ribbon at a right angle and twist it round twice, to form the centre. Secure at the bottom with a few stitches. Form the first petal by twisting the ribbon around the centre, folding it back at a right angle, so that the top edge lies across the "stalk", and catching it down with a secure stitch.

2 Continue to wrap the ribbon round in this way, securing each petal with a stitch. Finish off firmly, by stitching through all the layers.

3 Cut the green ribbon into 15cm/ 6in lengths and fold them to make leaves. Sew them to the centre of the hairband and then attach the rose in the middle.

4 Make six more roses in different colours and sew them along the hairband, interspersing them with more green leaves in both plain and gold-edged ribbon.

Join together vertical lengths of Fortuny-style pleated ribbon to make up a sculptural trinket bag. It's lined with iridescent fabric, and sparkling beads along the top edge add a pretty finishing touch.

Trinket Bag

you will need

1.6m/1⅝ yd pleated wire-edge ribbon, 50mm/2in wide

scissors

tape measure

dressmaker's pins

needle and matching sewing thread

40cm/16in pleated wire-edge ribbon, 56mm/2¼in wide

matching organza fabric

plate

pencil

sewing machine

38cm/15in fine matching cord

glass beads

1 To create the side of your trinket bag, cut the 50mm/2in-wide ribbon into eight pieces, with each piece measuring 20cm/8in in length. Now very neatly and firmly oversew the edges of these ribbon pieces together to form a tube.

2 For the bottom of the bag, simply stitch the two ends of the wider ribbon together.

3 Use a running stitch to gather one edge of the wider ribbon. Pull up the thread tightly and stitch to secure.

4 Slip-stitch the outer edge of the bottom of the bag to the lower edge of the side, turning in the raw edges.

5 For the lining, cut a rectangle 18 x 40cm/7 x 16in and a 14cm/5½in diameter circle from the organza. Use a suitable plate as a template.

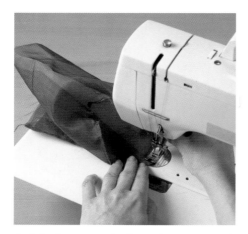

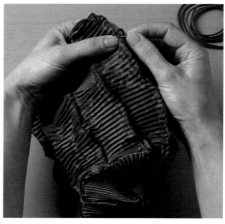

6 Machine-stitch the side seam, and pin and tack (baste) the side to the bottom of the bag. Machine-stitch together.

7 Fit the lining into the bag. Fold in the top edges of both the lining and the outer fabric and then slip-stitch the two together.

8 To make the carriers for the trinket bag's tie, cut two 6cm/2½in lengths of cord and poke the raw ends through a side seam on either side of the bag, 4cm/1½in from the top. Stitch securely in place. Now cut a piece of cord 25cm/10in long, fold it in half and knot the ends. Thread the loop through the tie carriers and pass the knotted ends through the loop.

9 As an attractive finishing touch, hand-stitch some decorative glass beads around the top edge of the bag at regular intervals.

This matching set is very easy to make in hooked ragwork. The domino spots, in loops of contrasting colour, stand out strongly against the cut pile background. Cotton jersey fabrics are ideal for this project.

Domino Hairslide and Earrings

you will need

pencil, ruler, card (stock) and scissors (for template)

30cm/12in square hessian (burlap)

felt-tipped pen

embroidery hoop

cotton jersey fabric in two contrasting colours

hook

scissors for cutting fabric

latex carpet adhesive

clear impact adhesive

10 x 4cm/4 x 1½in black felt (NB: extra will be needed for the earrings)

needle and matching sewing thread

hairclip fastening and earring clips

bonding adhesive

1 First, make yourself a card template that measures 10 x 4cm/4 x 1½in. Place it right in the middle of the piece of hessian and draw round it, using the felt-tipped pen. Now place the hessian piece in the embroidery hoop. Cut the jersey fabric into strips that measure 1cm/½in. Hook one of the colour blocks, making sure that you are working from the outside edge towards the centre.

2 Shear off the tops of the loops to create a cut pile surface. Repeat to make the second block of colour on the other half of the domino.

3 To make the spots for the domino, hook small loops in the contrasting colours. Do not cut these loops. Trim the excess fabric ends.

4 Remove the work from the hoop and place face down on a flat surface. Cut around the shape, leaving a border of 2cm/¾in all round. Apply a thin layer of latex adhesive over the back of the work and the border. Leave to dry for 5 minutes then turn in the border and press down firmly.

5 Apply clear impact adhesive to the back of the ragwork and cover with the black felt. Slip-stitch all round the edge. Attach the hairclip fastening to the back of the hairslide (barrette) using bonding adhesive and leave to dry for 1 hour. Make the earrings in the same way, using a 2.5cm/1in square template or a circle of the same size.

This set of hairslide (barrette) and hairbobbles is made from plastic carrier bags and remnants of nylon fabric! It shows what you can do at very little expense, and you can make the whole project very quickly.

Hooked Hair Accessories

you will need

pencil, ruler, card (stock) and scissors (for template)

25cm/10in square hessian (burlap)

felt-tipped pen

embroidery hoop

nylon fabric

scissors for cutting fabric

coloured plastic carrier bags

hook

latex carpet adhesive

12 x 6cm/4¾ x 2½in black felt

needle and matching sewing thread

clear impact adhesive

hairclip fastening

bonding adhesive

elastic hairbands

1 Make a sawtooth card template measuring 11 x 5cm/4½ x 2in for the hairslide (barrette). Place it in the centre of the hessian and draw round it with a felt-tipped pen. Put the hessian in the embroidery hoop.

2 Cut the nylon fabric and the plastic into strips 1cm/½in wide. Start by hooking the fabric to outline the marked area, working in rows.

3 Using the plastic, hook loops to fill in the central triangles. Bring the ends of the fabric and plastic strips through to the top of the work as you reach them. Trim any excess lengths.

4 Remove the hessian from the embroidery hoop. Place face down on a flat surface and cut round the shape, leaving a border of 2.5cm/1in. Apply a thin layer of latex adhesive over the back of the work and the border. Leave to dry for 5 minutes, then turn in the edges and press down firmly.

5 Lay the card template on the black felt, draw round it and cut out the backing. Apply clear impact adhesive to the back of the ragwork. Place the felt on the back of the hairslide and slip-stitch in position.

6 Carefully drop a small amount of bonding adhesive on to the top surface of the hairclip fastening, then hold it in position on the back of the hairslide. Leave to dry for 1 hour before wearing. Make the hairbobbles in the same way, using a round template of 2.5cm/1in diameter. Stitch the bobbles to the elastic hairbands.

This project uses a different ragwork technique to great effect. Fabric strips are wrapped round wire and bound with coloured embroidery threads, then coiled and sculpted into unusual brooches or earrings.

Wrapped Jewellery

you will need

three different fabrics

scissors

70cm/27½in wire

stranded embroidery thread (floss) in four colours, including a metallic thread

thick cotton thread

beads or sequins

pen or pencil

needle and matching sewing thread

brooch back

earring clips or wires

1 Cut the different fabrics into strips measuring 1cm/½in in width and the same length as the piece of wire. Starting at one end, wrap three different fabric strips round the wire, using embroidery thread to bind them in sporadic patches. When you are near the end of the wire, add a loop of thick cotton thread facing the end, and then continue wrapping the embroidery thread over this loop.

2 Thread the end of the embroidery thread into the loop with one hand, and with your other hand pull the two ends of the loop around until the thread end is tied off. Bind more embroidery thread in the other colours in patches along the length. Add a string of beads or sequins for extra decoration.

3 Wrap the metallic thread round one end, then wind it back on itself to tie in the end. Continue binding with the metallic thread, binding in the ends as before.

4 Wrap the finished bound length of wire around a pen or pencil to shape it into a spiral.

5 Remove the pen or pencil from inside the coiled length and sculpt it, working outwards and flattening it to make a cone shape. Stitch the fabric coils securely together and stitch on the brooch back. Make the earrings in the same way, but form the coiled lengths into lozenges instead of the cone shape. Stitch the earring findings to one end.

Even crisp (chip) packets can be hooked to make a loop pile surface just like fabric or yarn. In this heart-shaped brooch and matching ring the shiny plastic foil contrasts beautifully with the dark fabric border.

Crispy Brooch and Ring

you will need

pencil, card (stock) and scissors (for template)

30cm/12in square hessian (burlap)

felt-tipped pen

embroidery hoop

scissors for cutting fabric

dark fabric

hook

foil crisp (chip) packets

latex carpet adhesive

12cm/5in square black felt

clear impact adhesive

needle and matching sewing thread

brooch back and ring fitting

bonding adhesive

1 Make a card template for your crispy brooch by drawing a heart shape that measures approximately 8cm/3in across. Now place the card template on to your hessian square and draw round it, using the felt-tipped pen. Place the hessian into the embroidery hoop.

2 Cut the dark fabric into strips 1cm/½in wide. Begin the hooking by following the outline of the heart shape. Make the loops close together, approximately 1cm/½in high.

3 Cut the crisp packets into strips 1cm/½in wide. Fill in the centre of the heart shape with loops of the same height as the fabric loops. Bring all the ends through to the top of the work, and trim any excess lengths.

4 Remove the hessian from the embroidery hoop and cut around the shape, leaving a border of 2.5cm/1in. Apply a thin layer of latex adhesive to the back and the border and leave to dry for 5 minutes.

5 Using scissors, make snips in the border at regular intervals. Turn in the border and press down firmly. Draw round the template on the black felt and cut out the backing. Apply clear impact adhesive to the back of the work, then cover with felt. Slip-stitch around the edge.

6 Position the fastening on the back of the brooch and stitch, using double thread. Make the ring in the same way, using a 2.5cm/1in diameter circle for the template. Attach the ring fitting with bonding adhesive.

Pompoms are easy to make, and can be threaded with beads to make this colourful, quirky necklace. These pompoms are made from cotton yarn with a rich velvety finish, but mixing yarns is also effective.

Pompom Necklace

you will need

pair of compasses

pencil

stiff card (stock)

scissors

darning needle

cotton yarn in various colours

60cm/24in round cord elastic

multicoloured wooden beads

1 With compasses, draw two 4cm/ 1½in circles on the card with 2cm/¾in circles within them. Cut round the outer and inner circles

to form two card rings. Thread the needle with yarn. Hold the two rings together with the end of the yarn under your thumb, and wrap the yarn around the rings.

2 When the rings are covered and the centre space filled, insert the scissors between the two card rings and cut around them, through all the loops.

3 Insert a length of yarn between the rings. Wrap it several times around the cut strands, tie in a knot and remove the rings. Trim the pompom neatly and make seven more, in different colours.

4 Thread the needle with elastic and start a repeated pattern of stringing three beads on to the needle and then pushing it through a pompom. Finish by knotting the elastic and threading the ends back through the beads.

Natural vegetable-tanned leather can be moulded with your fingers when dampened and is used here to decorate a headband with flowers, which are easily coloured with permanent marker pens.

Floral Headband and Brooch

you will need

tracing paper, pencil, card (stock) and scissors (for templates)

scraps of vegetable-tanned, undyed leather

scissors for cutting leather

felt-tipped pens

sponge

PVA (white) glue

large brooch back

epoxy resin glue

elastic, 2cm/¾in wide

1 Following the templates at the back of the book, cut out all the elements for the headband and brooch from undyed leather. Using felt-tipped pens, colour in the leather "leaves" on the headband and brooch background. Using thin opaque pens, delineate outlines and markings on each flower. Then colour in with thicker translucent fluorescent pens.

2 Dampen all the elements with a moistened sponge, then shape the leaves and flowers with your fingers. Leave until completely dry. Scuff the surface of the leather on the headband and the brooch backing at the points of contact with the flowers. Then glue on the flowers with PVA glue. Attach the brooch backing with epoxy resin glue. Leave to dry.

3 Cut a V-shaped slot in each end of the headband backing. Cut the end of a piece of elastic into a point and slide it through one slot from front to back; glue into position with epoxy resin glue. Once dry, repeat with the other end, after trying on the headband to check the fitting.

The oak leaf motif is perfect for the warm autumnal colours of suede or leather. You'll need a tough piece of skin for the base layer of the hair ornament, but the buttons can be made from thin leather.

Oak-leaf Hair Clasp and Buttons

you will need

tracing paper, pencil, card (stock) and scissors (for templates)

pen

small, sharp scissors for cutting leather

small pieces of suede or leather in three colours

PVA (white) glue

stranded embroidery thread (floss)

sewing thread

small leather needle

glover's needle

pinking shears

hole punch

bamboo knitting needle

saw

abrasive paper

large self-cover buttons

1 Scale up the templates that have been provided for this project at the back of the book and then use them as guides to cut out two backing ovals and one front piece from different colours of either suede or leather. Now cut out your oak leaf stencil and then draw around it on to the top piece of suede.

2 Cut out the oak leaf shape from the suede using a pair of small scissors.

3 Glue the cut-out top piece on to the first backing piece using PVA glue. Leave to dry.

4 Stitch through the first backing piece with stranded embroidery thread to make a central leaf vein. Couch this down with sewing thread in a darker colour.

5 Using embroidery thread to match the backing leather and a glover's needle, make a running stitch border around the edge of the top piece.

6 Now neatly trim the edge of your first backing piece with the pinking shears. Then use more PVA to glue on the base layer. Once completely dry, use the pinking shears to trim the edge of this piece, too.

7 Carefully punch a hole at each side of the oak leaf using a No 6 hole punch. Saw a bamboo knitting needle down to a length approximately 5cm/2in longer than the hair clasp and rub the sawn end to a point with abrasive paper. Push the knitting needle down through one hole and out through the other.

8 Finally, to make the buttons, cut out circles of leather or suede large enough to cover the self-cover buttons. Cut out one oak leaf shape for each of the buttons from complementary colours of suede.

9 Glue each leaf to a backing circle. Lay a short length of stranded embroidery thread down the middle of the leaf and couch down with darker sewing thread.

10 Stretch the circle over the button dome, place the backing in position and snap it shut to secure.

The tradition of lucky wedding garters dates back many centuries. If you make this one using elements that are old, new, borrowed and blue, it should bring good luck to any bride!

Bride's Garter

you will need

10 x 90cm/4 x 36in pale blue silk

matching sewing thread

safety pin

50 x 3cm/20 x 1¼in elastic

1.5 x 5m/1½yd x 2in new lace

crystal rocaille embroidery beads

translucent blue and pearlized

6mm/¼in cup sequins

45cm x 3mm/18 x ⅛in light blue

satin ribbon

30cm x 6mm/12 x ¼in cream

satin ribbon

old button (for luck)

1 Sew together the long edges of the blue silk strip, leaving a 12mm/½in seam allowance. Turn it inside out by attaching a safety pin to one end and feeding it through the tube. Press lightly so the seam lies at the back.

2 Fasten the safety pin to the elastic and draw the elastic through the silk tube. Stitch the ends firmly together. Turn the raw edges of the silk under and oversew (overcast) the edges of the tube together.

3 Cut two 60cm/24in lengths of lace. Neatly join the ends of each piece to form a circle and decorate with beads and sequins, picking out the details of the lace pattern.

4 Run a gathering thread along each straight edge of lace and draw up to the same diameter as the garter. Even out the fullness, pin, and oversew the lace on to the silk.

5 Stitch the ends of the remaining piece of lace together. Gather tightly along the straight edge to form a rosette, and secure. Cut streamers of narrow blue and cream, satin ribbon and sew on to the back of the rosette.

6 Sew the rosette on to the garter and finish by decorating it with the old button for good luck.

Machine Embroidery

The versatility of machine embroidery enables needleworkers to experiment with a wide range of effects to produce truly original pieces. The great appeal of this craft is its speed – designs can be realized in a few hours and ideas captured with immediacy and spontaneity. Metallic threads are an ideal medium for this delicate form of jewellery: they can even be used on soluble material that is then dissolved to leave ethereal, glittering webs of stitches.

Most machine embroidery materials can be bought from craft suppliers. The most vital piece of equipment is, of course, a sewing machine, but it does not need a special embroidery programme.

Machine Embroidery Materials and Equipment

Darning foot

A darning foot is suitable for most embroidery, although fitting a presser foot gives a cleaner satin stitch. Alternatively, you can work without a foot, although the thread will tend to snap more frequently.

Embroidery hoops

A hand embroidery hoop can be used if the inner ring is wrapped in strips of cotton to hold the fabric taut. Special machine embroidery hoops with spring closures are more convenient.

Fabric

Calico provides a firm base for embroidery, but sumptuous fabrics such as shot organza, velvet and silk create a rich background. Felt can be used to back finished pieces.

Iron

Embroidery should be pressed on the wrong side to prevent scorching or flattening the stitches. Set a temperature that will not damage the least heat-tolerant part of the work.

Needles

Choose machine needles to match the thickness of the thread. Extra fine and metallic threads require 70/10 or 80/12 needles. For most other threads, 80/12 or 90/14 are suitable. Use a fine beading needle to attach tiny beads.

Non-woven interfacing

To stabilize fabrics for embroidery, back them with interfacing, which can later be torn away. Heavyweight interfacing can also be used alone as a base for filling stitchwork. Fusible interlining (interfacing) is used to bond layers of fabric together; templates can be drawn on the paper backing.

Sewing machine

The machine should have a free arm and a detachable bed for ease of movement. Make sure the feed can be lowered easily and that both top and bobbin tension can be adjusted. Clean and oil the machine regularly to keep it working smoothly.

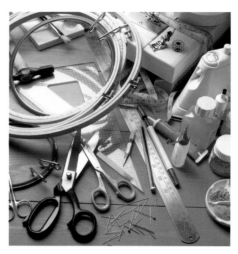

Thread

Machine embroidery thread is available in different weights. Metallic threads come in shades of gold, bronze, silver and other colours, sometimes twisted with matt threads for a more subtle effect. Be careful when stitching metallics at high speed as they occasionally snap. Use invisible thread to stitch beads on to embroidery.

Water-soluble film

Using a stabilizer while stitching prevents puckering and distortion of openwork and sheer fabrics. As an alternative to non-woven interfacing you can use water-soluble film, which pulls away after immersion in cold water or can simply be torn away or dabbed with water to remove it. It can also be used to create pieces of freestanding embroidery.

If your sewing machine is capable of zigzag stitch you can use it to create many different effects: all the designs in this chapter are achieved by varying basic stitches. Start by practising simple shapes and outlines.

Machine Embroidery Techniques

Preparation

On a domestic sewing machine the direction and size of the stitch are controlled by the presser foot and the feed. If these are both removed stitches of any size can be made. Many machines have a darning function that lowers the feed; on others, the feed should be covered and the stitch length set to 0.

The fabric needs to be stretched taut on an embroidery hoop. Place it right side up in the outer ring and press the inner ring over it so that it lies flat on the machine bed.

Stitching

Practise stitching with the machine set at a slow speed if possible. Set the stitch width to 0 and lower the presser bar to engage the top tension. Work a few stitches to secure the threads then trim the ends to stop them tangling. You can either manoeuvre the hoop or place your fingers either side of the foot to guide the fabric. Keep it moving steadily and practise stitching in every direction, working spirals and filling stitches, drawing and writing.

For regular stitching the tension should be even top and bottom, but interesting effects can be achieved by altering it. If you loosen the bobbin tension, for example, the top thread

will lie on the surface as if couched. Different textures and weights of fabric will also have an effect on the stitching.

Stitch problems

Oil the machine regularly and remove lint and threads from the bobbin case. If stitches are not properly formed or the threads break, check first that the machine is correctly threaded, the needle is correctly fitted and is not blunt or bent, and that it is the appropriate size for the thread.

If the needle breaks

Check that the top tension is not too tight. If the fabric is moved too forcibly it can bend the needle, causing it to hit the needle plate or bobbin case.

If the top thread breaks

Check that the top tension is not too tight, the top thread is not knotted and the presser bar is lowered.

If the bobbin thread breaks

Check that the bobbin tension is not too tight, the bobbin thread is evenly wound, and there are no threads caught in the bobbin case.

If the fabric puckers

Check that the tension is not too tight, the stitches are not too long, and the thread is not too thick for the fabric (if it is, use a stabilizer under it). If the needle is hitting the bobbin case, the timing may be out and the machine will need servicing.

Transferring designs

Start by creating a template, scaling up the design if necessary using graph paper or the enlarge facility on a photocopier.

1 Transfer the design to a piece of thin card and cut it out. Lay the template on the fabric and draw around it with a water-soluble fabric pen.

2 If a design cannot be drawn on the fabric because of its texture, trace it on to a piece of water-soluble film and pin this to the right side of the fabric. Dissolve after stitching.

Stabilizers

Light fabrics may be distorted during embroidery if they are not stabilized with a firmer backing.

1 For heavy embroidery pin non-woven interfacing or lightweight paper to the wrong side of the fabric. It can be torn away after stitching.

2 Use water-soluble film to support lightweight fabric, lace or openwork during stitching.

Appliqué

Fabric shapes cut out using a template can be appliquéd to the base fabric using a plain zigzag stitch.

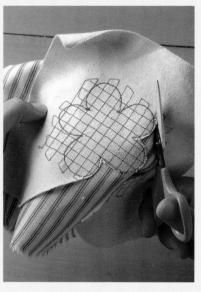

1 Draw the shape on the appliqué fabric, pin to the base fabric and stitch around the outline, then trim close to the stitching.

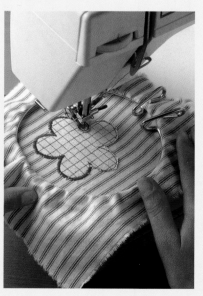

2 Or, draw the shape on fusible interlining (interfacing) and iron on to the base fabric. Cover the raw edge with zig-zag stitch.

Stitches These stitches will all be useful when making jewellery and related items. Practise them on spare scraps of fabric, and experiment freely with different threads and tensions to create original effects.

Whip Stitch

Loosening the bobbin tension and tightening the top tension produces a beaded effect as the bobbin thread is brought to the surface. It is most effective when the bobbin is threaded with a contrasting colour.

Zigzag Filler

Set the stitch width as desired and move the fabric from side to side. To add shading, work several rows of stitching making the edges jagged so that subsequent layers will blend into the previous ones.

Looped Stitch

Work whip stitch, tightening the top tension and loosening the bobbin. Remove the top thread with a needle and bond a piece of fusible interlining to the wrong side to hold the looped stitches in place.

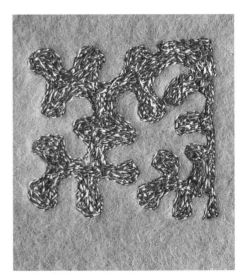

Couching

The fabric should be backed with a stabilizer. Lay a piece of thick thread or piping along the line of the design. Set the stitch width to the width of the piping and stitch down with a satin or zigzag stitch.

Satin Stitch

This can be worked in free embroidery or as regular stitching. Set the stitch width as desired; this can be varied along the line by altering the dial. Move the hoop slowly so that the stitches lie next to each other.

Double Threads

Thread two different threads through the needle together, using a large needle and a looser top tension to accommodate the extra thickness. This will give a subtle two-toned effect and tone down bright metallic threads.

Layers of contrasting fabrics and glittering machine embroidery make this a spectacular piece. The rough texture of the felts is wonderfully high-lighted by shimmering organza and metallic machine embroidery.

Sparkling Starfish Brooch

you will need

pencil, thin card (stock) or paper and scissors (for templates)

dressmaker's pins

purple felt

tailor's chalk

fabric scissors

rust felt

shot organza

sewing machine with darning foot

needle size 70/10–80/12

metallic machine embroidery thread

needle and matching sewing thread

brooch back

1 Draw two freehand starfish shapes on to thin card or paper, one larger than the other. Cut the templates out roughly. Pin the large starfish template to the purple felt and draw around it with tailor's chalk.

2 Cut out irregular pointed shapes from the purple and the rust felt. Pin them down along the points of the starfish outline. Cut out the smaller starfish shape from organza and pin it on top of the felt starfish.

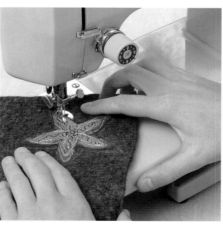

3 Thread the machine with metallic thread and stitch over the edges of the organza. Build up layers of texture and colour with different threads.

4 Cut out the felt starfish shape and a small circle of felt. Stitch this on to the centre back of the starfish. Stitch on the brooch back.

The heart is a timeless jewellery motif, evoking love and friendship. This filigree machine-embroidered hatpin, which can also be worn as a lapel pin, was inspired by baroque gilding found in a Czech church.

Heart Hatpin

you will need

water-soluble film

fabric pen

embroidery hoop

sewing machine with darning foot

needle size 70/10–80/12

metallic machine embroidery thread

thin jewellery wire

wire cutters

hatpin

beading needle

invisible thread

plastic beads in two sizes

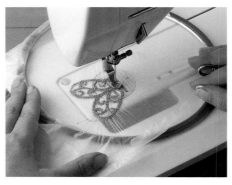

1 Copy the template from the back of the book, enlarging as required, and trace it on to water-soluble film with a fabric pen. Place the piece in an embroidery hoop and lower the sewing machine feed. Using metallic thread, stitch around the lines of the heart motif. Fill in the filigree outline, stitching in small circles.

2 Stitch back and forth several times over the circular stitchwork. Remove the work from the machine and turn the embroidery the other way up in the hoop.

3 Set a narrow zigzag width. Curve a length of jewellery wire around the stitched outline of the heart, starting and finishing at the point at the bottom of the heart. Couch the wire in place and trim the ends.

4 Remove the piece from the hoop. Lay the hat pin in the centre of the heart. Set a medium zigzag width and couch the pin in place.

5 Immerse the piece in cold water and pull away the film. Using a beading needle and invisible thread, stitch the beads around the edge of the heart. Sew through a large bead, then a small one and back through the large bead. Make a stitch in the edge of the embroidery to secure the beads.

This exotic character with his flamboyant headdress is embroidered using filling stitchwork in richly contrasting threads on a background of interfacing, and is designed for stitching on to a blazer pocket.

Blazer Badge

you will need

pencil, thin card (stock) and scissors
(for template)
20cm/8in square non-woven
heavyweight interfacing
fabric pen
fabric paints
paintbrush
iron
sewing machine with darning foot
needle size 80/12–90/14
coloured and metallic machine
embroidery threads
needle and sewing thread
embroidery scissors

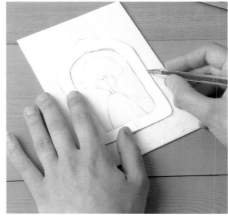

1 Follow the photograph opposite to draw the design, enlarging as required. Cut out a template from thin card. Lay this on a piece of interfacing and draw around the shapes with a fabric pen.

2 Using fabric paints, paint the background design in areas of solid colour, so that the white interfacing does not show through the stitching. Press with a medium-hot iron to fix the colours.

3 Lower the feed on the sewing machine. Fill in the design areas in the desired colours by working a straight stitch back and forth.

4 Work the face in a spiral from the centre point to the outline. To give a raised effect to the face, push the stitching out from the wrong side to form a dome shape.

5 Thread a needle with a dark thread and sew the eyes and nose details. Use gold thread to add the stars and the headdress details. Cut out the badge shape close to the outline. Set a medium stitch width and work a satin stitch all round the edge.

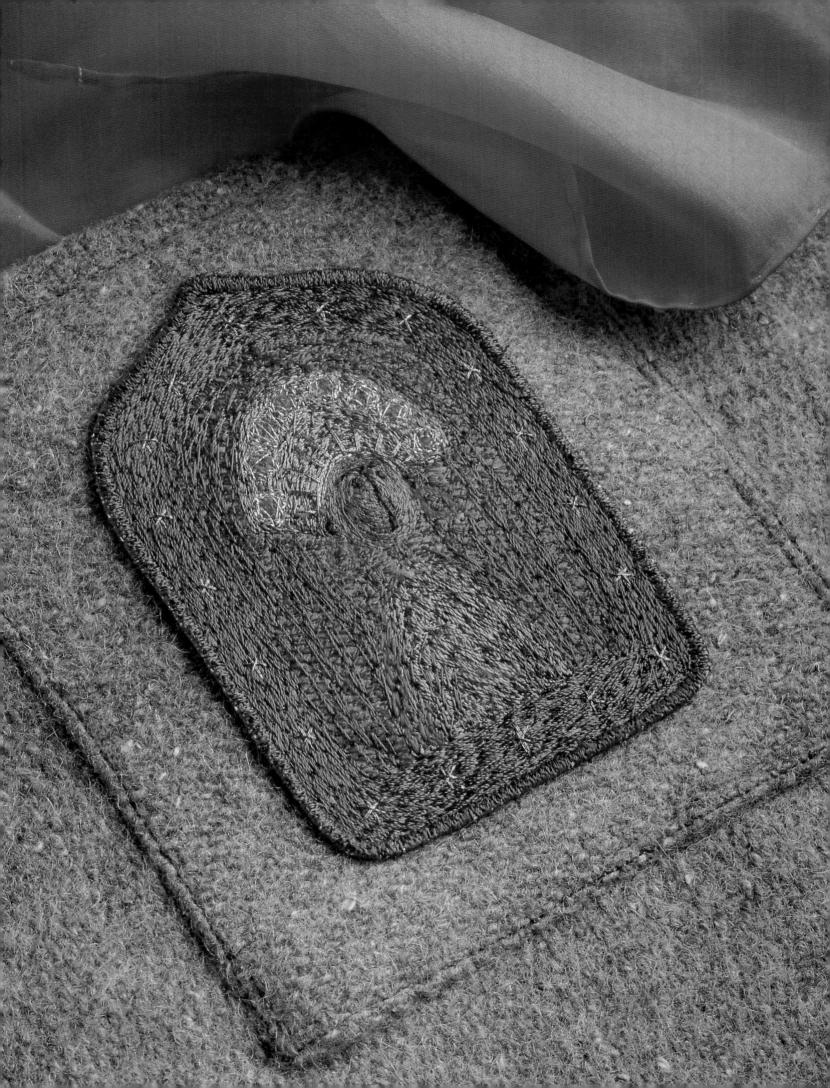

A decorative hatpin is a stylish way to jazz up a plain hat. This outsize brass pin is topped with an elaborate shining sun in machine-embroidered velvet, backed with rays of hammered metal.

Embroidered Sun Hatpin

you will need

yellow velvet

scissors

piece of any type of fine fabric

embroidery hoop

sewing machine with darning foot

needle size 80/12–90/14

coloured and metallic machine

embroidery threads

brass sheet

tin snips

metal file

small ball hammer

brass wire

wire cutters

round-nosed (snub-nosed) pliers

epoxy resin glue

glass beads

hatpin

1 Cut out a yellow velvet sun. Place a piece of fine fabric in an embroidery hoop (to act as a stabilizer) and machine-stitch the sun to it. Thread the machine with contrasting threads in the top and bobbin and whip-stitch around the edge. Then make a deeper decorative band of stitching around the edge. Stitch a spiral on each ray in contrasting threads and finish with the face in the centre. Trim the velvet sun away from the fine fabric.

2 Cut out a larger sun shape from the brass sheet using tin snips, and file the edges until smooth. Hammer the brass to give it some interesting texture. To make an enclosure for the hatpin, form a spiral at each end of a piece of wire and hammer flat. Centre the wire over the brass sun and glue in place. Cut out a small circle of brass and glue over the wire.

3 Now glue the velvet sun on to the centre of the brass sun. Thread some glass beads on to the hatpin and glue them in place at the end. To assemble the finished piece, bend the wire spirals slightly backwards so that you can easily slide the hatpin through the top and bottom spirals.

A winged horse makes a stunning brooch, with subtle glints of light in the embroidery hinting at precious metal. The three-dimensional form is created after stitching and the back is varnished to hold the shape.

Horse Brooch

you will need

tracing paper, pencil, paper or card (stock) and scissors (for templates)

20cm/8in square calico

scissors for cutting fabric

water-soluble film

dressmaker's pins

embroidery hoop

sewing machine with darning foot

needle size 90/14

metallic and coloured machine embroidery threads

small piece of velvet

fine cord

acrylic varnish and paintbrush

beading needle

invisible thread

beads

brooch back

1 Copy the templates from the back of the book, enlarging as required. Cut the horse and wing shapes out of calico and pin them on to a piece of water-soluble film. Now place the piece in an embroidery hoop.

2 Lower the feed on your machine and stitch around the edges of the shapes. Cut some velvet to the shape of the horse's body and pin it in place. Fill the bobbin with contrasting thread and use two threads in the needle: one metallic and one coloured. Stitch over the velvet randomly to hold it in place.

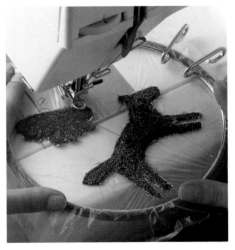

3 Fill in the wing area in a contrasting metallic thread. Stitch over the raw edges of each shape in small circles to neaten them.

4 Curve a length of fine cord around the outline of each shape. Set a medium zigzag width and couch the cord in place.

5 Set the stitch width to 0. Work a narrow band inside the couched cord in a contrasting colour.

6 Take the embroidered pieces out of the hoop and immerse in cold water. Pull away the water-soluble film and leave to dry.

7 Stitch one end of the wing on to the horse's back using thread of a matching colour.

8 Shape the horse and the wing by curving them over your hand. To hold the shapes, paint two coats of acrylic varnish on to the wrong side of the pieces. Allow to dry.

9 Thread your beading needle with invisible thread and stitch small beads around the edges of the wing. Stitch a larger bead on to each hoof. Finally, stitch a brooch back on to the wrong side of the piece.

The intensely coloured ground fabric of this bracelet contrasts wonderfully with metallic embroidery in a strong, simple geometric pattern, embellished with embroidered domes topped with beads.

Harlequin Bracelet

you will need

pencil, ruler, paper or card (stock) and scissors (for template)

scissors for cutting fabric

30cm/12in square silk

fabric pen

iron

dressmaker's pins

non-woven interfacing

embroidery hoop

sewing machine with darning foot

needle size 80/90–12/14

metallic and coloured machine embroidery threads

embroidery scissors

metallic fabric paint

paintbrush

white paper

small coin

water-soluble film

beading needle

invisible thread

beads

brass jewellery wire

wire cutters

file

round-nosed (snub-nosed) pliers

clasp fastening

needle and matching sewing thread

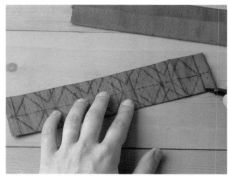

1 First, cut out a paper or card template to the size required and then use this card template to cut out two pieces of silk, making sure that you leave a 2.5cm/1in seam allowance all around the edge. Now draw the pattern on to one of the pieces of silk with a fabric pen. Turn under the seam allowance on both pieces and press.

3 Working carefully, cut away the interfacing close to the machine stitching. Now paint diagonal lines between the stitched areas with your metallic fabric paint. Press the piece between two completely clean sheets of white paper, in order to fix the metallic paint.

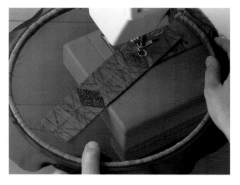

2 Pin the patterned fabric to a piece of non-woven interfacing and place in an embroidery hoop. Lower the feed on the sewing machine. Fill the bobbin with contrasting thread and use a metallic thread in the needle. Using whip stitch, fill in each diamond and triangle shape, working in a spiral from the centre to the outside edge.

4 Use a coin to draw four circles on water-soluble film. With metallic thread on top and coloured thread in the bobbin, work back and forth from a circle's centre to its outline, then work a spiral from centre to outline. Immerse the piece in cold water, pull off the film and press each circle into a dome.

5 Thread a beading needle with invisible thread and sew a bead to the pinnacle of each dome. Stitch each dome at four points around its base over the point where two diamond shapes meet.

6 Cut seven pieces of jewellery wire 10cm/4in long. File the ends smooth and twist a spiral at each end using round-nosed pliers. Set a medium zigzag width and, using metallic thread, couch the wires on to the bracelet, one through each diamond and one at each end of the bracelet.

7 Pin the second piece of silk to the embroidered piece, wrong sides together. Set the stitch width to 0 and work a line of stitching all around the edge. Hand-stitch a clasp fastening to the ends of the bracelet.

These embroidered diamond-shaped earrings are padded to make them three-dimensional while remaining extremely light. A rich combination of colours and textures gives a precious, jewel-like quality.

"Diamond" Earrings

you will need

pencil, paper or thin card (stock) and scissors (for template)

fabric pen

small pieces of calico

small pieces of organza and silk

dressmaker's pins

sewing machine with darning foot

needle size 80/12

embroidery hoop

coloured and metallic machine embroidery threads

small, sharp scissors for cutting fabric

wadding (batting)

PVA (white) glue

2 small paintbrushes

metallic acrylic paint

needle

2 eye pins, 2 metallic beads and 2 glass beads

round-nosed (snub-nosed) pliers

earring wires

1 Cut out a diamond-shaped stiff paper or card template to the required size, and then use it to draw two diamond shapes on to the calico. Now draw four horizontal lines across each diamond, using a fabric pen. Pin a piece of organza over each marked shape. Lower the feed on the sewing machine and place the fabric in an embroidery hoop. With matching thread, stitch the horizontal lines and several lines around the design.

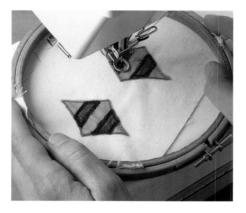

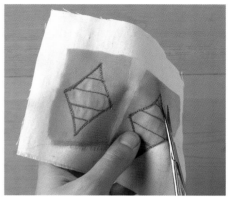

▲ **2** Now, working very carefully, use your scissors to trim away the excess organza, cutting close to your stitched outline.

◀ **3** Cut two pieces of silk in a contrasting colour. Pin them over the diamonds. Place the piece in a hoop. Stitch some lines around the horizontal stripes with matching thread. Trim off excess fabric close to these lines. Work lines of stitching around the stripes to cover raw edges, plus more lines around the design with metallic thread.

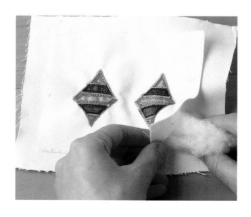

◀ **4** Pin a second piece of calico to the wrong side of the embroidery. Place it in the hoop and stitch around three sides of each diamond. Stuff both diamonds with wadding, right into the corners. Close up the fourth side with stitching. Cut out the shapes close to the stitched outline. With a brush, apply PVA glue to the edges of the shapes to varnish and stiffen them. Leave to dry.

5 Now paint the back and the edges of the diamond shapes, using metallic acrylic paint. When the paint has dried, make a hole at the top of each diamond with a needle. Thread each eye pin through a small metallic bead, a glass bead and then the embroidered diamond. Using round-nosed pliers, twist the wire at the back to secure in place and attach the earring wires to the eye pins.

This unusual fan-shaped comb is decorated with deeply worked embroidery. There are no solid areas of colour, but a subtle, densely mottled surface created by whip stitching one colour over another.

Glittering Hair Comb

1 Copy the templates from the back of the book, enlarging as required, and draw around them on to the calico. Now cut out the fabric pieces and pin them to water-soluble film. Place the whole piece in an embroidery hoop. Lower the feed on the sewing machine. Using contrasting threads in the bobbin and the needle, work whip stitch in circles to fill in the outline. Stitch areas of different colours bleeding into each other to give a mottled effect. Stitch in circles to neaten the raw edges.

◄ **3** Immerse the pieces in cold water and pull away the film. Cut a 2.5cm/1in square of card and eight 1m/1 yd lengths of jewellery wire. Wrap a length of wire around the card. Cut the wire at one end and twist the strands together at the other end to make a tassel. Repeat with the other lengths. Set a medium zigzag width and, using metallic thread, couch the tassels in place between the points on the larger piece of embroidery.

2 Turn the piece over in the hoop. Fill the bobbin with metallic thread and use contrasting thread in the needle. Work a whip stitch along the zigzag edge of the larger piece.

4 Lay the smaller piece on top of the larger, matching up the lower edges. Set the stitch width to 0 and join the two pieces using matching thread, stitching in circles. Hand-stitch the top bar of the hair comb to the lower edge of the embroidered piece. Draw around the larger template on to a piece of self-adhesive felt and cut out the shape. Peel off the paper backing and stick the felt on to the back of the embroidery.

This stunning necklace features cords that appear to be wrapped but are in fact embroidered. Unusually shaped beads picking up a colour in the stitchwork are suspended between the cords on jewellery wire.

Beaded Necklace

you will need

sewing machine with darning foot

needle size 90/14

fine metallic and coloured machine embroidery threads

40cm/16in and 72cm/29in lengths thick cord

60cm/24in thin cord

pencil, stiff paper or thin card (stock) and scissors (for template)

pen

felt

scissors for cutting fabric

dressmaker's pins

water-soluble film

embroidery hoop

pin board

needle and matching sewing thread

round-nosed (snub-nosed) pliers

brass jewellery wire

wire cutters

beads

necklace clasp

1 Lower the feed on the sewing machine. Fill the bobbin with a metallic thread and use a coloured thread in the needle. Set a medium to wide zigzag width and feed each of the cords through the machine several times, changing the colours each time to give a mottled effect. Create bobbles at intervals along the cords by stitching back and forth over a point with metallic thread.

2 Draw a heart shape approximately 1cm/½in tall on thin card. Use this template to draw four hearts on a piece of felt and cut them out. Pin the felt hearts on to a piece of water-soluble film and place in an embroidery hoop. Set the stitch width to 0 and fill in the shapes with whip stitch, spiralling outwards from the centre to the edge. Immerse the piece in water and pull away the film.

3 On a pin board, pin out the shortest length of cord to make the inner ring and the medium length 2cm/¾in from the first to make the outer ring. Pin the longest length of cord around the outer ring, making curves along its length. Hand-stitch the points where the curves meet the outer ring. Using pliers, bind the ends of the cords

together with brass jewellery wire. Cut 22 pieces of wire, each 5cm/2in long, and thread a bead on to each one. Using pliers, twist one end of each wire around the inner cord and the other end around the outer cord. Attach some of the beaded wires between the curved cord and the outer ring. Trim the ends of the wires.

4 Cut four 6cm/2½in lengths of wire. Use a needle to pierce a hole at the top and bottom of each embroidered heart. Thread each wire through a bead, then through the heart and through another bead. Twist the ends of each wire into spirals and attach both ends to the cords. Hand-stitch the clasp to the ends of the cords.

Metallic threads, iridescent paper and shimmering beads combine to make these glittering pieces of jewellery. The embroidery is done on a base that dissolves to leave only the sparkling tracery of stitches.

Iridescent Earrings and Pendant

you will need

water-soluble film

embroidery hoop

dressmaker's pins

tracing paper, pencil, stiff paper or thin card (stock) and scissors (for templates)

fabric pen

iridescent paper

sewing machine with darning foot

needle size 90/14

metallic machine embroidery threads

general-purpose scissors

iron

kitchen paper

self-hardening clay

stiff wire

blue-green watercolour inks

paintbrush

metallic paints

card

felt

plastic sheet

acrylic spray varnish

beading needle

selection of small beads

2 split rings

pliers

2 jump rings

earring wires or posts

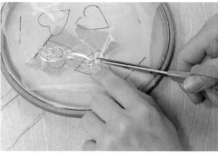

1 Stretch a layer of water-soluble film in an embroidery hoop and then pin another layer to the back. Copy the templates provided at the back of the book, enlarging them if necessary, and draw round them on the film. Now pin pieces of iridescent paper to the back of the film over the centres of the motifs. Thread the bobbin and needle with metallic thread. Set the machine stitch width to 0 and lower the feed. Work stitching in circles around the centres of the motifs and then carefully cut away any excess iridescent paper from the back.

4 Make small balls of self-hardening clay for the beads, and push them on to a stiff wire. Leave to dry, stuck into a piece of clay.

2 Machine-stitch right around the outlines of the motifs, and then fill in the area around the centres with whip stitch, spiralling outwards to the edge.

3 Immerse the embroidery in water to dissolve the film. Iron dry between kitchen paper.

5 Paint the clay beads with blue-green watercolour inks. Leave to dry, then add highlights with dots of metallic paint.

6 Cover a large piece of card with felt and then with plastic sheet, to make a soft backing sheet. Pin the motifs to the backing and coat the clay beads and the embroidered motifs with acrylic spray varnish.

7 Using a beading needle, attach metallic thread to the top of a motif. Thread on two small beads, then a clay bead and two more small beads. Take the thread through a split ring and then back down again through the beads and into the motif. Fasten off. Sew a ring of small beads around the centre of the motif.

8 To make an earring, open a jump ring with pliers and thread through the split ring. Join it to the ring on the earring wire or post. If you are making a pendant, then thread a machine-embroidered chain through the slip ring.

A jewellery roll should be part of every jewellery-lover's luggage set. This luxuriously padded and embroidered velvet version is specially designed to safeguard its contents when travelling.

Jewellery Roll

you will need

23 x 33cm/9 x 13in polyester wadding (batting)

23 x 33cm/9 x 13in velvet for outer layer

matching sewing thread

tissue paper

23 x 10cm/9 x 4in metallic organza

metallic machine-embroidery thread

1.6m x 18mm/1¾yd x ¾in ribbon

20cm/8in zip (zipper) in matching colour

23 x 48cm/9 x 19in contrasting velvet for lining

press studs (snaps)

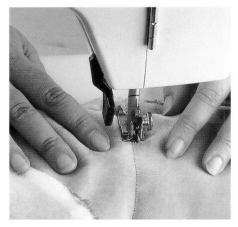

1 Tack (baste) the wadding (batting) to the wrong side of the outer fabric, smoothing carefully. Sew together round the outside edges and straight stitch across the width 9cm/3½in from the left edge.

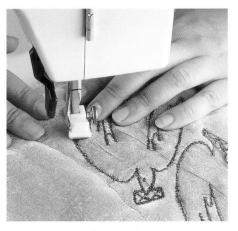

2 Draw your chosen design on to tissue paper. Tack the organza to the right side of the velvet and the tissue paper to the wrong side, 9cm/3½in from the left edge. Straight stitch over the pencil line, working from the wrong side. Turn the piece over, cut back the excess organza, then zigzag stitch over the outline on the right side, using metallic thread.

3 Cut a 23cm/9in length of ribbon and stitch one side of it to the left edge. Fold over to enclose the raw edges and slip stitch to secure.

4 Cut another 23cm/9in length of ribbon and, using a zipper foot, attach to one side of the zip. Sew the ribbon edge to the other side of the zip.

5 Turn under the same allowance along the edge of the lining velvet, then stitch the upper edge of the ribbon to the lining.

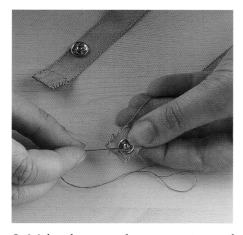

6 Make the strap from two pieces of ribbon, 20cm/8in and 10cm/4in long. Turn under one end of each piece, enclosing the raw edges and securing with tiny slip stitches. Attach press studs (snaps) to the neatened ends. Pin the raw ends to the lining 6mm/¼in from the zip, and join the press studs together in the middle.

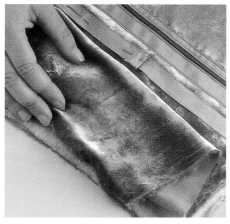

7 Make the pocket section by folding the right side of the overlapping lining inwards and then turning it back on itself. Adjust until the pockets are 7.5cm/3in deep.

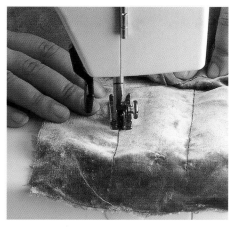

8 Stitching lengthways, divide the fold up into four separate pockets, sewing through the layers of the lining only.

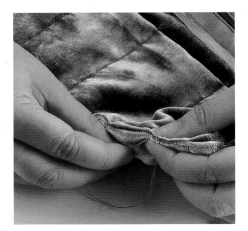

9 Turn under the raw edges on the right side and oversew (overcast) the lining to the outer fabric, to enclose the edges. Bind the top and bottom sides with ribbon as shown in Step 3. Machine-stitch one edge and catch down the other selvage with slip stitch. Tuck the ends in and oversew.

10 Make ties from two or four pieces of ribbon 25cm/10in long. Turn under one raw edge on each piece and oversew two to the roll as show above, or four as shown in the main picture. Trim the loose ends into a 'V' shape.

Beads and
Shells

Strings of beads are perhaps the simplest, most primitive form of personal adornment, but they are infinitely adaptable, and new ways of decorating with beads are constantly being devised. Modern beads are available in an enormous range of materials, shapes and textures, from glass and metal to semi-precious stones. Shells, which are beautiful natural objects in their own right, are equally versatile starting points for inspirational jewellery designs.

Many craft suppliers specialize in beads, and finding a particularly beautiful example is often the inspiration for a piece of jewellery. Only a few other basic materials are needed for most projects.

Beadwork Materials and Equipment

Bead loom

This small loom is specially designed for use with beading thread, and enables you to weave narrow bands of small beads in colourful patterns. They can be turned into items such as bracelets and headbands. The warp threads are wound around wooden rollers at each end of the loom and fitted between metal springs to space them evenly.

Beading needles

Fine, long beading needles can be used to thread several beads at a time, so are particularly useful when working with tiny beads. They need careful handling as they break easily.

Beading thread

Fine, strong nylon thread is specially designed for beadwork, though a strong smooth thread such as polyester may be equally effective. Large beads can also be threaded on decorative yarns such as silk.

Beading wire

Gold, copper and silver wire are available in many gauges: 0.4mm (gauge 30 or 25) and 0.6mm (gauge 22) are the most useful. Check that the wire will fit through the holes in the beads.

Beads

Glass – Glass beads are available in every colour and size, from tiny seed beads and rocailles to large, decorated Venetian and drop beads. Small beads are sometimes sold pre-strung: this makes them easy to transfer to a beading needle, but they are also ideal for stitching down in couched designs.

Indian lampwork beads sometimes have an insert of foil and are decorated with molten glass patterns. To make wound beads, molten glass is wound around a rotating metal rod to create swirling striped patterns.

Metal – These beads often have sophisticated shapes and are made in copper, brass and other alloys; they

may also be plated with gold or silver. Small metal spacer beads are often used to separate larger beads or at the end of a string.

Natural materials – Mother-of-pearl, bone and wooden beads are all available in many shapes and sizes.

Beeswax

Waxing beading thread strengthens it and helps to prevent it snagging on sharp edges, which is especially useful when threading faceted beads.

Cord

Threaded small beads can be wrapped around a core of three-ply piping or furnishing cord to make chunky pieces of jewellery.

Cotton spheres

These and other shapes made of compressed cotton fibres are available from beading suppliers.

Self-cover buttons

Sold in kit form in a range of sizes, these can be covered with fabric on to which beads can be stitched.

Fabric paint

If fabric is used as a foundation for beadwork, it may need to be coloured to match the beads. For small projects a permanent fabric pen can be used.

Glue

Epoxy resin glue or a glue gun can be used to attach small beads.

Palettes

Decant beads into white china artist's palettes or saucers to keep colours separate and make them easier to pick up.

Round-nosed (snub-nosed) pliers

Jewellery pliers are essential for shaping wire in small coils and for opening and closing rings and other findings.

Scissors

An old pair of scissors can be used to crack damaged or misplaced beads so that they can be removed from a string without unthreading all the others.

Tweezers

These are useful for both selecting and removing very small beads.

Shells are found in an amazing variety of shape, size, colour and texture, making them a fascinating craft medium. Stylish modern jewellery designs are an ideal setting for their natural, subtle beauty.

Shellwork Materials and Equipment

Assorted shells

Beautiful shells have been keenly collected for centuries, and their desirability has inevitably led to their exploitation in trade. Taking attractive and sometimes rare shells from their natural habitat – perhaps with their original owners still inside them – can result in the depletion of marine species. Consequently, shell-collection and export has now been made illegal in some parts of the world. It's important to make sure that any shells you use have been gathered in a responsible way.

Beachcombing is an enjoyable activity when you are at the seaside, and huge drifts of small shells can sometimes be found washed up along the beach. In these circumstances a small number can safely be collected as long as you make sure they are empty when you pick them up.

Other environmentally sound sources of shells include fish dealers and restaurants and old shell necklaces and other craft items. If you eat shellfish such as cockles and mussels at home you can simply save the shells; otherwise they are regularly discarded

by restaurant kitchens and if you make friends with your local seafood restaurant the staff may be happy to save some for you.

Old shell necklaces and trinkets are a very good source of small shells for jewellery-making, with the advantage that the shells are already drilled for threading. They're cheap and easy to find at flea markets and jumble sales.

Dust mask

Always wear a mask when sanding shells to avoid inhaling the dust.

Glue

A glue gun is useful for attaching shells quickly and accurately, but epoxy resin glue or PVA (white) glue are also suitable. Epoxy putty comes in two parts that are mixed together just before use. It is a strong adhesive that can be used to fill small shells to take button backs and other fittings.

Goggles

Wear protective goggles when drilling or sanding shells.

File

Use a small file to smooth any rough edges on shells that might catch on skin or clothing.

Ink

To colour shells, inks containing shellac are ideal. They can be mixed or watered down to achieve subtle shades and are waterproof once dry.

Mini-drill

A small electic drill is the most useful tool you can invest in for any kind of shellcraft. The very small bits will enable you to drill tiny holes in the most fragile of shells. Other attachments are available for smoothing surfaces, grinding rough edges and polishing shells until they shimmer.

Reusable putty adhesive

Press shells into a blob of putty on the work surface to hold them securely while you are drilling them.

Ribbons

Choose ribbons with a seaside feel – such as checks and stripes in fresh colours – for shellcraft projects, or use delicate pinks and creams to match the colours of the shells.

Stone-effect beads

Natural-looking beads in a variety of shapes combine well with shells.

Tweezers

A pair of tweezers may be helpful for picking up and positioning tiny shells.

When threading beads or shells, it's important that the thread you choose is strong enough to support their weight. Shells need to be drilled for threading, and may be polished to enhance their natural beauty.

Bead and Shellwork Techniques

Pre-strung Beads

Small glass beads are often supplied pre-strung, making them ideal for creating pieces such as rope necklaces or for attractive couched designs.

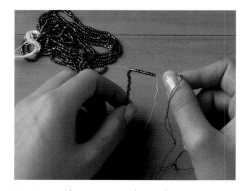

1 In order to re-thread pre-strung beads, thread a beading needle and pass it through the beads. Once you have the length that you need, then simply remove the old thread from the string.

2 For a couched design, lay a length of pre-strung beads down on a piece of fabric following the line of a design. Now stitch over them, positioning your stitches between the beads, to secure.

Threading a Bead Loom

Bead weaving produces narrow, flat strips of beaded fabric. The beads lie between the warp threads, and a continuous weft thread is passed through the beads, weaving over and under the warp threads.

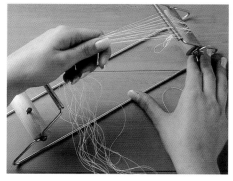

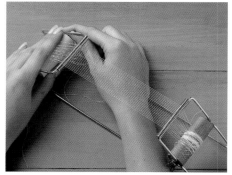

1 Cut the warp threads to the length of the finished piece plus 45cm/18in. Cut one thread for each bead across the width, plus one extra. Lay the threads out smoothly and knot them at each end. Divide the strands in half and slip one knot over the rivet in the roller. Wind on the threads then arrange them evenly in the spring.

2 Slip the knot at the other end of the warp threads over the rivet in the other roller and wind on as before until the warp threads are taut.

3 Thread a beading needle with a long length of thread and draw it through beeswax. Tie the end of the thread to the first warp thread 2.5cm/1in from the roller.

Needle-woven Beading

In this beading technique, a continuous thread is taken through successive rows of beads, with the second row fitting between pairs of beads in the first. The second row is joined to the first by interweaving. For a long piece such as a necklace that does not need a clasp, the work can be done in rounds; for shorter pieces work the second row in the opposite direction to the first. Additional rows can be added in the same way, woven into the preceding row of beads.

1 Thread on the required number of beads for the first row. Knot the ends of the thread if working in rounds.

2 Pass the needle through the first bead of row 1, then through the first bead of row 2, then the third bead of row 1. Repeat to the end of the row.

Sanding and Polishing Shells

1 Using a coarse sanding disc on a mini-drill, remove the outer coating of the shell and smooth down the ridges.

3 Use a woolly mop head to shine the inner surface of the shell.

Amazing results can be achieved by sanding and polishing ordinary shells such as these green mussels. Always wear a dust mask and goggles.

2 Switch to a fine sanding disc to strip the shell down to mother-of-pearl (the shell will now be very fragile).

4 To get into the corners, use a conical felt mop.

Drilling Shells

A mini-drill can be used to make holes in small shells. The more fragile the shell, the finer the bit should be and the slower the drilling speed.

Before you start drilling, secure each shell to the work surface with reusable putty and hold it firmly in place as you work. Judging the right place to make a hole is often a matter of instinct.

These delicate gold wire earrings take the form of tiny sets of scales filled with beads in shades of green and blue. Thread the same number of beads into each basket so that the scales balance.

Beaded Balance Earrings

you will need
fine brass beading wire
fine crochet hook
round-ended pencil
selection of small glass beads
round-nosed (snub-nosed) pliers
4 jump rings
2 split rings
earring posts with loops
and butterfly backs
20 gauge/0.8mm/0.03in brass wire
wire cutters

1 Using the fine brass beading wire, crochet four round shapes that measure 1cm/½in across. On the last round make three 2cm/¾in equally spaced loops. Leave a long end of wire. Twist the loops.

2 Mould each round into a dome shape over the end of a pencil. Thread equal numbers of beads on to the loose end of wire and secure them in each basket. Do not trim the wire yet.

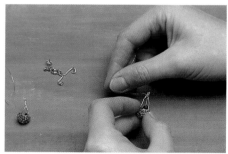

3 Using pliers, attach a jump ring, then a split ring, to each earring fitting. Cut two 4cm/1½in lengths of the 20 gauge wire. Twist an upward loop in the centre of each, then bend the ends down into two loops from which the baskets will hang. Attach the centre loop to the split ring using another jump ring. Thread the long end of wire on one basket through the top of the twisted loops to bring them together and attach to the bar. Repeat with the other baskets. Trim the ends of the wire.

Ornate hatpins were once an indispensable fashion accessory, as no lady would venture out without a hat. These contemporary versions could be worn on a lapel if you don't need them to hold a hat in place.

Ornate Beaded Hatpins

you will need

decorative and diamanté beads

hatpin bases with safety ends

glue gun or clear impact adhesive

lengths of ribbon in several colours, 6mm/¼in wide

needle and matching sewing thread

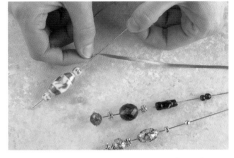

1 Choose a selection of beads in matching or complementary colours and in various shapes and sizes. Pick out a small bead to put on the pin first to prevent the others slipping off the end. Smear the shaft of the pin with a very thin coat of glue, then add the other beads.

2 Streamers can be added by threading a length of narrow ribbon between the beads. Tie into a bow and secure with a few stitches.

3 To create a flowered effect, twist lengths of narrow ribbon into a few tiny roses. Sew a few stitches through the base of each flower to secure, then glue the roses between the beads.

In this sumptuous creation, multiple strands of beads are joined at intervals with large Venetian beads – this is an ideal way to show off a few precious beads by mixing them with small beads in toning colours.

Venetian Necklace

you will need
beading needle
scissors
strong black nylon thread
5mm/³⁄₁₆in lilac iridescent and red
glass beads
3mm/¹⁄₈in bronze and green
glass beads
7 large Venetian glass beads
2 crimping beads with loops
round-nosed (snub-nosed) pliers
2 x 5mm/³⁄₁₆in gold loops
S-shaped gold fastener

1 Thread a needle with 250cm/100in of nylon thread and knot the ends together. Tie a bead to the end, as an anchor. Thread beads on the double thread as follows (just a suggestion, those seen opposite are different): one lilac, 25 bronze, one green, two bronze, two green, one red, three green, one red, one lilac, one Venetian, one lilac, one red, three green, one red, two green, two bronze, one green. Repeat the sequence six more times. End with 25 bronze beads and a lilac one.

2 Cut another 250cm/100in length of thread, thread through the needle, knot and tie around the anchor bead as before. Pass the needle through the first lilac bead threaded in step 1 then thread on 25 bronze, one green, two bronze, two green, one red and three green. Pass the needle through the red, lilac, Venetian, lilac and red beads threaded in step 1. Repeat this sequence six more times, ending with 25 bronze beads and passing the needle through the last lilac bead.

3 Make another three interwoven strands in the same way. Tie the threads in a tight knot at each end, then attach a brass crimping bead over each knot and close with pliers.

4 Attach a gold loop to the top of each crimping bead. Thread the fastener through the loops.

Small plastic boxes with well-fitting lids can be used to keep all kinds of small treasures safe. Recycle one with style, jazzing it up with glass paints in strong colours and a sprinkling of tiny, glittering seed beads.

Glittering Trinket Box

you will need

clear plastic box

black relief outliner

ruler

flat-backed gold bead

all-purpose glue

small glass beads

glass paints in dark brown, crimson and yellow

medium and fine paintbrushes

kitchen paper

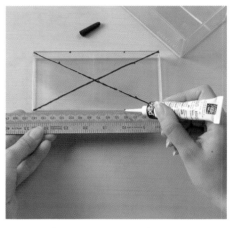

1 Mark out a simple geometric pattern on the lid of your box, using black relief outliner. Use a ruler to make sure that you keep all of your lines straight.

2 Rest the outliner on the ruler to guide it when you are outlining the edge of the lid.

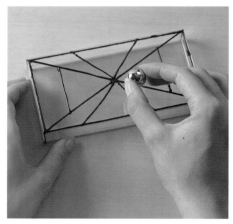

3 While the outliner is still wet, press a flat-backed gold bead into the centre. As it dries, the outliner will hold the bead securely in place.

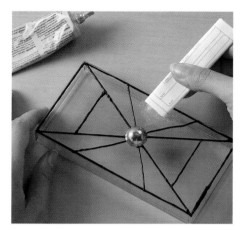

4 Cover the four panels on the cross on the lid with a thin layer of all-purpose glue.

5 While the glue is wet, sprinkle small glass beads on to the surface and let them stick.

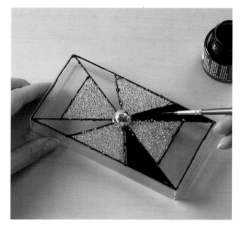

6 Fill in the areas between the beaded panels on the lid using the dark brown glass paint.

7 Paint the remaining areas on top of the lid in crimson.

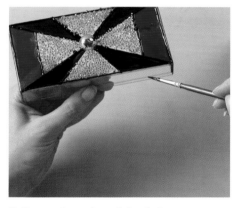

8 Paint the sides of the lid in crimson, and leave to dry.

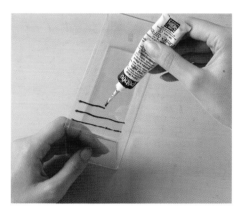

9 Using black outliner, draw vertical lines down the sides of the box at 1cm/½in intervals.

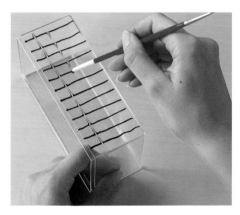

10 Immediately, drag the pointed end of a paintbrush through the lines to break them up. Drag the brush in alternate directions at 1cm/½in intervals down the sides, wiping the excess paint off the brush at the end of each stroke. Leave for at least an hour to dry.

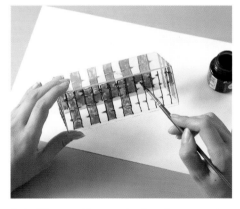

11 Use a fine paintbrush to paint alternate stripes in crimson along the sides of the box.

12 Paint the remaining stripes around the sides in bright yellow and leave to dry completely.

Cord beading, in which strings of small beads are wound around and then stitched on to a readymade cord core, is very popular with the Zulu people, who are among the world's most skilled beadworkers.

Cord-beaded Bracelet

1 Bind both ends of the cord tightly with thread to stop them unravelling. Paint the cord with fabric paint in a colour that matches the beads, so that it will not show through.

2 Thread the needle and make a few stitches at one end of the cord. Thread on 20 beads, holding the thread taut and pushing the beads together. Wind the beads around the cord, make a couple of stitches then pass the needle back through the last few beads. Repeat along the length of the cord.

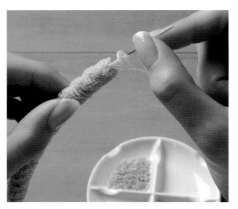

3 To finish the ends of the cord, thread on a few beads and make a stitch across the blunt end. Make several more stitches to completely cover the end.

4 Make a beaded loop at one end of the cord large enough to fit the button. At the other end, thread on three beads then pass the needle through the button. Thread on two more beads, pass the needle back through the button and make several stitches to finish off.

This pretty scalloped tiara is heavily encrusted with spirals of artificial pearls. The backing is stiffened with wire and stitched to a hair comb, and the tiara would be ideal to hold a bridal veil in place.

Pearl Tiara

you will need

tracing paper, pencil, card (stock) and
scissors (for template)
non-woven heavyweight interfacing
fabric pen
scissors for cutting fabric
17.5cm/7in millinery wire
round-nosed (snub-nosed) pliers
needle and matching
sewing thread
beading needle
beading thread
1cm/½in pearl bead
6mm/¼in pearl beads
4mm/⅕in pearl beads
4 x 8mm/⅖in pearl beads
4 drop pearl beads
plastic hair comb

1 Copy the template from the back of the book on to card, scaling up as necessary, and cut out. Place your card template on to the interfacing, draw around it twice, and cut out. Bend a loop at each end of the millinery wire. Now stitch the wire to one piece of the interfacing 2cm/¾in from the straight edge.

2 Following the template guide, mark the centre of each scallop on the right side of the wired interfacing. Stitch the 1cm/½in pearl bead to the centre of the middle scallop. Bring the needle through to the right side next to it and thread on eight 6mm/¼in beads and enough 4mm/⅕in beads, spiralling outwards, to fill the scallop shape, then make a fastening stitch to secure.

3 Thread a sewing needle with matching thread and make tiny stitches over the beading thread in between the pearl beads. Repeat for the other scallops, using 8mm/⅖in beads in the centre of each. Couch down the small beads to fill in all the remaining areas of interfacing.

4 Slip-stitch the back piece of the tiara to the front. Stitch the drop beads between the scallops.

5 Stitch the comb to the back of the tiara, catching it along the bottom edge of the beaded piece.

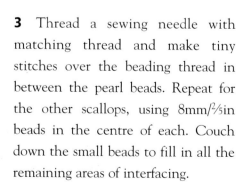

The starting point for this necklace was the unusual filigree pendant at the centre. The beads are strung on a length of knotted silk, created by working blanket stitch around a core of thread.

Chinese Necklace

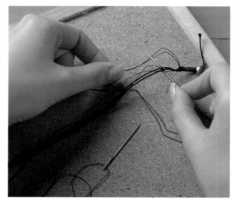

1 For each side of your Chinese necklace, cut a 1m/1 yd length of 2-ply silk thread. Fold in half and pin the midpoint to a pinboard. Cut two 2m/2 yd lengths of fine silk. Thread each on to a large-eyed needle, double the thread, tie a knot and slip both knots over the pin. Lay the fine silk thread next to the 2-ply lengths. Work a blanket stitch along the threads for 12cm/4½in.

2 Now carefully separate the 2-ply silk strands and, using the two needles and the fine silk, work a blanket stitch for 2.5cm/1in down each strand individually.

3 Thread a bone bead on to one strand and a round amber bead on to the other. Tie double knots just beneath the beads. Continue as for step 1 for another 1.5cm/⅝in.

4 Thread on a round lampwork bead and tie a knot just beneath it. Continue as one strand for 1.5cm/⅝in, divide in two for 1.5cm/⅝in, thread on two precious stone beads, tie knots.

5 Continue as two strands for 1.5cm/⅝in, join and continue as one strand for 1cm/½in, thread on a lampwork disc, knot, continue as one strand for 1cm/½in. Thread on a bone, a large amber and another bone bead, knot, and continue as one strand for 1cm/½in. Make the other side of the necklace to match. Tie the two sides together, thread all ends through the large pendant and knot.

6 Thread the ends through a lampwork disc and knot. Thread the ends back through the disc and trim. Remove the piece from the board and stitch the necklace clasp to each end.

Satisfying to make, any of these lovely buttons would add a unique touch to a special garment. The luscious blackberry would look equally attractive as a pendant hanging from a bracelet or necklace.

Beaded Buttons

you will need

black felt-tipped pen

1cm/½in diameter compressed cotton sphere

needle and matching sewing threads

small black glass beads

vanishing fabric pen

3cm/1¼in and 1.5cm/⅝in diameter self-cover buttons

silk

scissors

large transparent glass beads with silver-lined holes

4mm/³⁄₁₆in green crystal beads

taffeta

5mm/³⁄₁₆in green glass bead

small copper-coloured glass beads

small transparent glass beads

1 For the blackberry button, use a black felt-tipped pen to cover the cotton sphere completely. Thread a needle with black sewing thread and make a few stitches at the top of the sphere to secure the end.

2 Thread on a small black glass bead, make a stitch then pass the needle right through the sphere. Thread on another bead and stitch down. Take the needle around the sphere, passing through the two beads at top and bottom, then around at right angles to divide it into quarters.

3 Thread on 18 beads and pass the needle through the bead at the bottom of the sphere. Thread on 18 more beads and pass the needle through the top bead. Repeat, taking more beads around the sphere at right angles.

4 Thread on 16 beads and work from top to bottom as before, this time dividing the sphere into eight sections. Repeat with 14 beads, dividing the sphere into 16 sections, until the whole sphere is covered.

5 If the blackberry is intended to hang on a bracelet or necklace, secure a thread at the bottom and thread on eight beads. Insert the needle back into the sphere at the same point to make a loop.

6 For the flower button, use a vanishing fabric pen to draw around the 3cm/1¼in self-cover button on to the silk. Draw another circle 1cm/½in larger and cut out. Mark five equally spaced points around the inner circle.

7 Thread a needle and fasten the thread at the centre of the circle. Thread on 20 large transparent glass beads, then insert the needle back at the same point to make a loop.

8 Bring the needle out at one of the points marked on the circle. Couch down the loop at this point with a stitch between the tenth and eleventh beads. Make four more glass-bead petals in the same way.

9 Stitch a green crystal bead in the centre of the flower.

10 Run a gathering stitch 3mm/⅛in from the raw edge. Place the self-cover button in the centre of the silk and pull up the gathering thread. Secure with a few small stitches and attach the back of the button.

11 For the tassel button, draw around a 1.5cm/⅝in self-cover button on to a piece of taffeta, then draw another circle 7mm/⅜in larger and cut out. Thread a needle and fasten the thread in the centre of the circle. Thread on a green glass bead and eight copper beads, then pass the needle back through the green bead and fasten off. Gather the raw edges and cover the button as in step 10.

12 For the jewel-encrusted button, draw around a 1.5cm/⅝in self-cover button on to a piece of taffeta, then draw another circle 7mm/⅜in larger and cut out. Run a gathering stitch around the edge and cover the button as in step 10. Thread a needle and fasten the thread in the centre of the button. Thread on a green crystal bead and some small transparent glass beads, then pass the needle back through the green bead. Make another stitch and repeat until the button is completely covered.

These richly decorative earrings are made of card tubes covered in velvet ribbon then wrapped with metallic thread and gold wire studded with beads. All the larger beads are attached with hatpins.

Wrapped Earrings

you will need

thin card (stock)

pencil and ruler

scissors

velvet ribbon, 5cm/2in wide

needle and matching sewing thread

red metallic embroidery thread

textured gold wire

wire cutters

beading needle

matching beading thread

small green glass beads

4 hatpins

8 x 4mm/^{3}/$_{16}$in brass flower beads

8 x 6mm/^{5}/$_{16}$in red glass beads

12 x 4mm/^{3}/$_{16}$in red glass beads

round-nosed (snub-nosed) pliers

4 x 7mm/^{3}/$_8$in hexagonal brass beads

silver earring wires

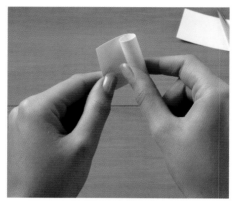

1 Cut two 4 x 7cm/1½ x 2¾in rectangles of card. Starting from one short side, roll each into a narrow tube 1.5cm/⅝in in diameter.

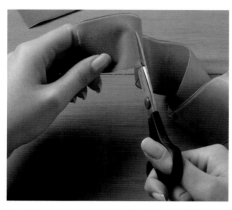

2 Cut two pieces of velvet ribbon 6 cm/2½in long. Roll a piece of ribbon around each card tube, right side out.

3 Fold under the raw edges of the ribbon and slip-stitch the seam. Thread a needle with red metallic thread, double it and knot the end. Fasten it to the end of a tube, wrap it evenly up the tube to the other end and fasten off.

4 Cut 40 pieces of textured gold wire, each 1.5cm/⅝in long. Thread a beading needle with beading thread and fasten to the end of a tube. Thread on pieces of gold wire and small green glass beads alternately. Wrap the beaded thread around the tube between the strands of metallic thread and fasten off at the other end. Wrap the second tube to match.

5 Push a hatpin through each tube 5mm/¼in from the top so that the ends are of an equal length each side. Thread a flower bead, a large red bead and three small red beads on to each side. Twist the ends into spirals, snipping off the excess if necessary.

6 Taking another hatpin for each tube, thread on a brass bead, a large red bead, a hexagonal bead, the wrapped tube, then the same beads in reverse. Trim each hatpin end and bend into a loop. Attach earring wires to the top loops.

Inspired by the designs of the Art Deco movement, the geometric pattern of this bracelet is worked in pearlized ice-cream colours. The piece is worked in small glass beads on a bead loom.

Woven Bracelet

you will need

tape measure

beading thread

scissors

bead loom

beading needle

beeswax

small light green, pink, grey and purple glass beads

adhesive tape

wool lining fabric

needle and matching sewing thread

3 buttons with shanks

1 Measure your wrist to determine the length of the bracelet and add an extra 45cm/18in. Cut 21 warp threads to the total length. Lay out the threads and knot together at one end. Divide evenly into two strands. Slip the knot over the roller rivets of the beading loom. Wind on the threads a little by turning the roller, then spread the threads out and arrange one in each coil of the spring.

2 Tie a knot in the other end of the warp threads. Slip this over the rivet in the other roller with approximately half the threads on each side as before, and wind on. Arrange the threads in the corresponding coils of the other spring and wind the rollers on to adjust the tension – the warp threads should be taut.

3 Thread a beading needle with a long thread and draw the thread through beeswax. Tie the end of the thread to the far left warp thread 2.5cm/1in from the roller. Thread on 20 beads, pushing them up as far as they will go and fitting them between the warp threads.

4 Push the beads up through the spaces between the warp threads, and pass the needle back through the beads above the threads. Pull the thread tight. Thread on 20 more beads and repeat.

5 Continue, following the pattern at the back of the book. When complete, finish off the weaving by passing the needle back through several rows of beads. Tie a knot and trim the thread.

6 To remove the work from the loom, cut two lengths of adhesive tape and stick them firmly over the unbeaded warp threads at either end of the work. Cut the threads near the spring.

7 Cut a piece of wool lining fabric to the same size as the finished work. Tuck the free warp threads under and assemble the work and the lining with the wrong sides together. Now work a slip stitch all around the finished piece.

8 On one end of the bracelet, stitch three buttons at equal distances. Make three beaded loops in corresponding positions at the other end, large enough to fit over the buttons.

We tend to think that Victorian colours were always dark and sombre, but this beautiful embroidered and beaded jewellery was reproduced from original 19th-century pieces displayed in a costume museum.

Victorian Earrings and Brooch

you will need

tracing paper, pencil, card (stock) and scissors (for templates)

30cm/12in square cream cotton fabric

embroidery hoop

needle and matching sewing thread

stranded embroidery thread (floss) in pale green and warm pink

invisible thread

beading needle

tiny crystal beads

iron

30cm/12in square fusible interfacing

30cm/12in square satin lining

small scissors for cutting fabric

brooch back

earring wires

1 Copy the templates provided at the back of the book and then transfer the designs to your cream cotton fabric. Fit the cotton material into an embroidery hoop. Begin embroidering the brooch shape at the outer edge. Using three strands of green thread, work four rows of chain stitch. Work three rows in pink thread, followed by four more rows in green.

2 Fill the centre of the brooch with beads. Now iron the interfacing on to the wrong side of the satin lining and use the template to mark out the shape of the brooch.

3 Cut out the brooch and the lining, with a 1cm/½in seam allowance around each piece. Trim the corners, snip the curves and turn in the edges. Slip-stitch the backing to the embroidery.

4 Sew a loop of five beads on to each point of the brooch using a double thread, and finish off securely. Stitch on the brooch back.

5 Make the earrings in the same way, but add extra loops of beads in between the points. At the top of the earrings thread on four beads and an earring hook and bring the thread back through the beads before finishing off securely.

This regal purple box is covered in jacquard silk and lined with delicate lilac lightweight silk. The lid is quilted, following the fabric's pattern, and beaded with sparkling starburst motifs to highlight the design.

Jewellery Box

you will need

sheet of 6mm/¹⁄₄in foam-core board

cutting board

metal ruler and craft knife

50 x 90cm/20 x 36in toning lightweight silk

PVA glue

adhesive tape

20 x 40cm/8 x 16in calico

thin card (stock)

30 x 90cm/12 x 36in of silk

jacquard fabric

clothes pegs (pins)

matching embroidery silks

1m x 90cm/40 x 36in polyester wadding (batting)

embroidery hoop

assortment of small beads

1 Draw up the six box pieces on to the foam-core board: two 15 x 20cm/6 x 8in rectangles for the lid and base; two 7.5 x 20cm/3 x 8in sides and two 7.5 x 14cm/3 x 5½in ends. Cut out on a cutting board using a metal rule and a craft knife. (If you want different dimensions, adjust the pieces as required and allow more or less fabric as appropriate).

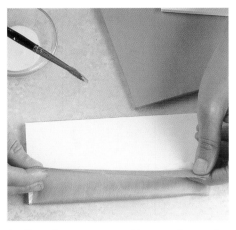

2 Cut four pieces of lining from the lightweight silk, slightly larger than each side and end. Using PVA (white) glue, stick the fabric along each side about halfway down, stretching it tightly. When nearly dry, turn the board over and stretch the silk across the top edge, gluing it to the back. Trim the silk close to the board, leaving a short overlap at each corner. Cover the base piece with lining fabric in the same way.

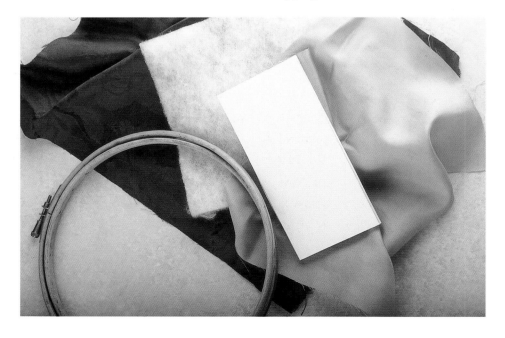

3 Spread glue along the base of one long side, and along the base and edge of one end. Place the base right-side up and position the two sides around the corner of the base. Glue and place the other two sides around the opposite corner. Use adhesive tape to keep the joints tight while the glue dries. Use a pin to push the silk overlaps at the top corners down into the cracks.

4 Draw the hinge on to calico: the base should be the width of one long side, plus one end, with the 'flap' slightly smaller than the box lid. Cut the flap sides at an angle as shown. Glue to the box back and around the sides, leaving the flap at the top.

5 From thin card (stock), cut three rectangles the same size as the front and two sides of the assembled box. Cover each piece with silk jacquard, then glue to the front and sides of the box, holding the fabric in place with clothes pegs (pins) while the glue dries.

6 With embroidery silk, overstitch the joins at the box corners, then return along each line of stitching to form cross stitches.

7 Cut a 25 x 33cm/10 x 13in piece of jacquard to cover the lid and a piece of wadding (batting) slightly larger than the lid itself. From the lightweight silk, cut out an 18 x 23cm/7 x 9in rectangle. Sandwich the layers together as shown and put into an embroidery hoop, stretching the fabric tightly.

8 Make French knots in a harmonizing colour, stitching through all three layers and picking out details of the jacquard pattern, or creating a random effect. Keeping the piece in the embroidery hoop, quilt the fabric by hand or machine, outlining the shapes within the material.

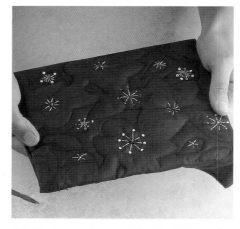

9 With a contrasting colour and single stitches, sew star shapes around the French knots. Sew beads around the outer edges of the stars, and embroider additional stars in any spaces.

10 Position the card for the lid on the wrong side of the embroidery and trim the wadding and backing as necessary. Glue the front face-down, stretching the fabric firmly, then stretch and glue the two sides, neatening or mitring the corners. Allow to dry thoroughly.

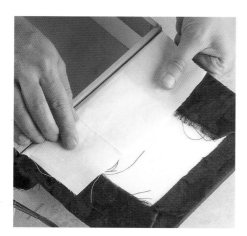

11 Stick the calico hinge to the underside of the lid so that the lid lies squarely on the box when closed. Cut a piece of card the same size as the back of the box, less 3mm/⅛in in depth to allow the lid to open properly. Cover with jacquard silk as before. Making sure that the front is flush with the box, glue the back flap of the embroidered lid to the back of the box, then glue on the jacquard-covered card. Embroider the corners, as in Step 6, then glue the upper long side of the inner hinge to the inside of the lid.

12 Cut a piece of thin card slightly smaller than the lid of the box, cover it with lightweight silk, then glue in place on the underside. Cut a piece of card and wadding 12mm/½in smaller all around than the box lid and lightly glue them together. Stretch and glue the silk over the wadding, then stick the card in the centre of the underside of the box lid. Make a centre divider from a silk-covered piece of foam-core board 1cm/⅜in lower than the walls. Pad the inside of the box by covering and padding pieces of card to fit each wall, as for the inside lid, and glue in place.

Typically Victorian, this butterfly decoration would look most elegant on a simple black dress. It could also be pinned to a belt in the place of a buckle, or even used as a hair ornament for a special occasion.

Butterfly Brooch

you will need

20cm/8in square closely woven
black fabric

vanishing fabric pen

embroidery hoop

beading needle and black
sewing thread

scissors

20cm/8in square black felt

mounting (mat) board

double-sided tape

large round iridescent beads

large and small long black beads

large and small round black beads

craft (utility) knife

cutting board

latex adhesive

brooch back

1 Transfer the butterfly design provided with the templates at the back of the book on to the black fabric using a fabric pen, and fit the material into an embroidery hoop. Thread the needle with a double thread and knot the end.

3 Cut out the butterfly, leaving a 1cm/½in border. Trim the corners and snip into the curves. Using the template, cut butterfly shapes from felt and mounting board. Score down each side of the body on the board. Cut double-sided tape to fit round the edge and stretch the beaded fabric on to the board.

2 Sew on the large round, iridescent beads individually to make the eyes and highlights of the wings. Outline the body with large long beads and the wings with shorter beads, then fill in the rest of the butterfly with small round beads.

4 Use latex adhesive to glue the felt shape on to the back of the butterfly. When dry, stitch bead feelers on to the head: take the needle though a long bead, then a round bead, then back through the long bead on each side. Stitch the brooch fastening on to the back. Now gently bend the wings forward.

Buttons can easily be made from all sorts of shells, as long as there is a means of attaching them. They look especially effective on clothing made from natural fabrics, such as wool and cotton, in neutral colours.

Snail-shell Buttons

you will need

protective gloves

epoxy putty

small snail shells

small eyelet screws

wire cutters

file or abrasive paper

needle and matching button thread

1 Wearing protective gloves, mix together the two parts of the epoxy putty. Push putty into the mouth of each snail shell and fill the spiral recesses on the back of the shell. Smooth the surface with your finger.

2 Press a small eyelet screw into the putty on the back of each shell. If the screw is too long for the depth of the shell, snip off the end with wire cutters before inserting it.

3 Leave the putty to dry, then file or sand smooth, making sure there are no sharp edges at the mouth of the shell. Sew the shell buttons on to the garment with a needle and matching button thread.

Combine the contemporary look of corrugated cardboard with a dynamic shell arrangement. For the finishing touch, paint the box in pure white, and the result is a seashell box that resembles a meringue-topped cake.

Seashell Jewellery Box

you will need

selection of seashells

round corrugated cardboard box with lid

glue gun

paintbrush

white acrylic gesso or paint

1 Sort the seashells into different shapes and sizes. Arrange them on the lid of the box, using some larger shells as the bottom layer of the design.

2 When you are happy with the arrangement, begin to glue the bottom layer on. Glue the outside shells first, and gradually move inwards.

3 Work with the shell forms, building the middle of the design up into a domed shape.

4 Paint the box and the lid white. If you are using acrylic gesso, two coats will give a good matt (flat) covering; ordinary acrylic paint will benefit from an extra coat.

Rainbow cockle shells in pretty, variegated colours are stitched on to a coloured cord to make this simple necklace. The long trimmed ties at the back make it a perfect accessory for beachwear or a backless dress.

Cockle-shell Necklace

you will need

rainbow cockle (small clam) shells

coloured cord

reusable putty adhesive

mini-drill

file

stranded embroidery thread (floss)

embroidery needle

epoxy resin glue

2 small winkle shells

1 Select an odd number of cockle shells and arrange them around the cord with the largest one in the centre at the front of the necklace.

2 Supporting each shell on a lump of reusable putty adhesive, drill a small hole through the top. File any rough edges smooth.

3 Stitch the shells on to the cord using embroidery thread.

4 Apply epoxy resin glue to the ends of the cord and insert each one into a small winkle shell.

The shell used to make this romantic locket is called a heart cockle because of its shape. It opens naturally down the middle, revealing a chamber large enough to conceal a message or small memento.

Valentine's Locket

you will need

heart cockle shell

reusable putty
adhesive

mini-drill

pink stranded embroidery
thread (floss)

embroidery needle

pleated satin ribbon

scissors

PVA (white) glue

small mementoes

fine silk ribbon

1 Holding the shell steady on a piece of reusable putty adhesive, drill a small hole through the top of each half through which to thread the ribbon.

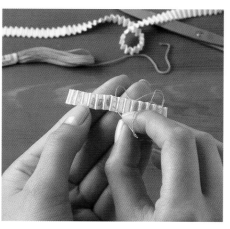

2 Using pink embroidery thread and an embroidery needle, stitch the words "I love you" inside the pleats of a small piece of pleated satin ribbon.

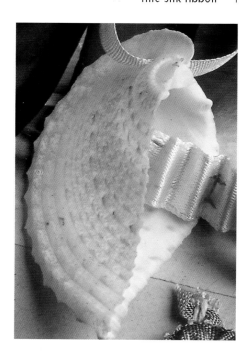

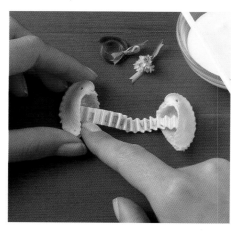

3 Glue one end of the ribbon inside each half of the cockle shell and leave to dry. Tuck the ribbon inside and insert small mementoes such as a lock of hair and a photograph.

4 Close the shell and thread a fine silk ribbon through the holes at the top of the shell. Wrap the ribbon around the shell to hold it closed.

Patterns for some of the projects are given here so you can make templates. The way you copy these may depend on the materials being used, but cutting out a card template and drawing round it is often the best approach.

Templates

Tracing

Unless you have access to a photo-copier, you will need to trace the printed pattern before transferring it to a piece of card for cutting out.

Scaling up

You may want to make a template that is larger than the printed design. Scaling up is easily done using a photo-copier with an enlarging facil-ity, but failing this you can use graph paper. For very small designs, scaling down may be required.

1 Use a pen or pencil to draw over the image. Turn the tracing over on a piece of scrap paper and use a soft pencil to rub over the lines.

2 Place the tracing, right side up, on a sheet of paper or card (stock). Using a hard pencil, draw firmly over all the lines of the design.

1 Trace the design and tape the tracing over a sheet of graph paper. Using an appropriate scale, draw the design on a second piece of graph paper, copying the shape from each small square to each larger square.

3 Lift off the tracing to reveal the design. Go over the lines if necessary before cutting out the template.

4 When working with fabric, it may be possible to trace the design directly using a fabric pen. Tape the drawing to a light box or window and tape the fabric over it to hold it still while you draw.

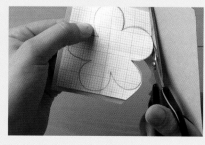

2 Lay or paste the graph paper template on a sheet of card and cut around the outline.

Fabric and Leather Templates

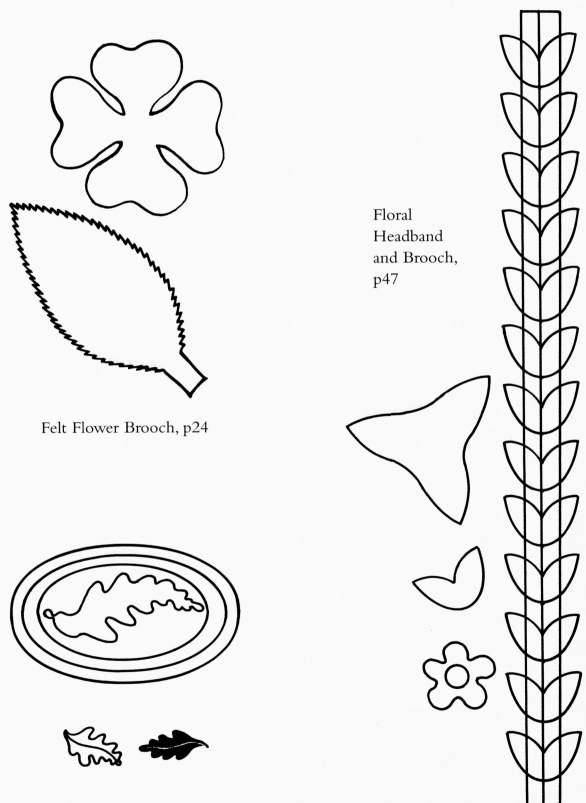

Felt Flower Brooch, p24

Floral
Headband
and Brooch,
p47

Oak-leaf Hair Clasp and Buttons, p48

Machine Embroidery Templates

Heart Hatpin, p60

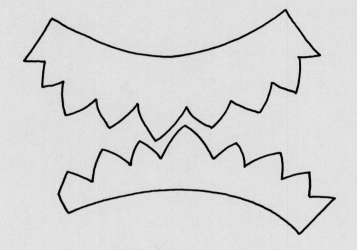

Glittering Hair Comb, p72

Horse Brooch, p65

Iridescent Earrings and
Pendant, p76

Beads and Shells Templates

Pearl Tiara, p98

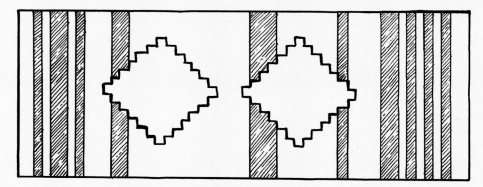

Woven Bracelet, p108

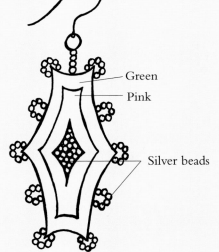

Green

Pink

Silver beads

Victorian
Earrings and
Brooch, p110

Fill in background with small beads

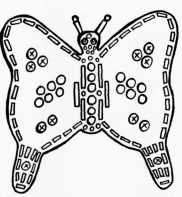

Beads marked with a cross are
black iridescent beads; all others
are plain black beads

Butterfly Brooch, p116

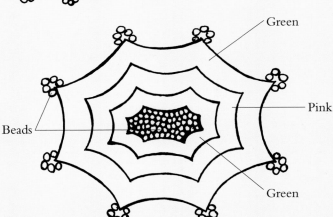

Green

Pink

Green

Beads

Index

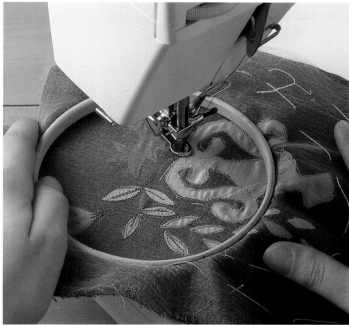

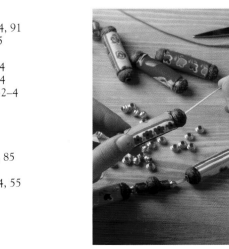

Acknowledgements

The publishers would like to thank the following craftspeople for designing the projects in this book. Apologies to any people who may, unintentionally, not be credited.

Victoria Brown:
Felt Bead Necklace p20, Felt Bracelet p22, Felt Flower Brooch p24, Marbled Earrings p26, Acorn Buttons p28, Pearl Tiara p98

Louise Brownlow:
Iridescent Earrings and Pendant p76, Beaded Balance Earrings p90

Judy Clayton:
Ribbon Beads p30, Embroidered Sun Hatpin p64, Wrapped Earrings p106

Lucinda Ganderton:
Rose Hair Accessory p32, Ribbon Rose Hairband p34, Bride's Garter p49, Ornate Beaded Hatpins p91, Venetian Necklace p92

Alison Harper:
Victorian Earrings and Brooch p110

Angela Harrison:
Wrapped Jewellery p42

Susie Johns:
Glittering Trinket Box p94

Julie Johnson:
Pompom Necklace p46

Mary Maguire:
Floral Headband and Brooch p47, Oak-leaf Hair Clasp and Buttons p48, Snail-shell Buttons p117, Cockle-shell Necklace p119, Valentine's Locket p120

Abigail Mill:
Sparkling Starfish Brooch p58

Lizzie Reakes:
Domino Hairslide & Earrings p38, Hooked Hair Accessories p40, Crispy Brooch & Ring p44

Isabel Stanley:
Trinket Bag p35, Heart Hatpin p60, Blazer Badge p62, Horse Brooch p65, Harlequin Bracelet p68, "Diamond" Earrings p70, Glittering Hair Comb p72, Beaded Necklace p74, Jewellery Roll p78, Cord-beaded Bracelet p96, Chinese Necklace p100, Beaded Buttons p102, Woven Bracelet p108

Isabella Whitworth:
Jewellery Box p112

Dorothy Wood:
Butterfly Brooch p116

Photography
The publishers would like to thank the following photographers for their work on the featured projects:

Karl Adamson
Lisa Brown
Steve Dalton
Nicki Dowey
James Duncan
John Freeman
Michelle Garrett
Janine Hosegood
Tim Imrie
Gloria Nicol
Lizzie Orme
David Parmiter
Debbie Patterson
Debi Treloar
Peter Williams

Thanks also to the authors, stylists and illustrators whose work is featured in this book.